A TALE OF TWO COURTS

JUDICIAL
SETTLEMENT
OF CONTROVERSIES
BETWEEN
THE STATES
OF THE SWISS
AND AMERICAN
FEDERATIONS

A TALE OF TWO COURTS

WILLIAM GORHAM RICE

THE UNIVERSITY
OF WISCONSIN PRESS
MADISON
MILWAUKEE
AND LONDON
1967

PUBLISHED BY
THE UNIVERSITY OF WISCONSIN PRESS
MADISON, MILWAUKEE, AND LONDON
U.S.A.: BOX 1379, MADISON, WISCONSIN 53701
U.K.: 26–28 HALLAM STREET, LONDON, W. 1

PRINTED IN THE UNITED STATES OF AMERICA
BY KINGSPORT PRESS, INC.
KINGSPORT, TENNESSEE
LIBRARY OF CONGRESS
CATALOG CARD NUMBER 67–20758

PREFACE

THIS brief account of how the chief courts of two nations, the one sitting in English-speaking Washington in a common law environment and the other located in French-speaking Lausanne and operating within a legal system of Roman origin, have utilized their authority in an area of controversy between very distinguished suitors, has none of the Dickensian flavor that its title suggests. No fiction here; no heartbreaking episodes; only the record of an exploration of functionally similar judicial territories in different continents to discover their likenesses and diversities. This, like *The Tale of Two Cities*, is the story of a small drama within a large drama. For it is not a full view of the two courts, but only an exposition, and to a degree an appraisal, of their achievement in a legal area in which few national courts operate—the settlement of disputes that arise among powerful political corporations: between the component states and commonwealths of the United States of America, and between the cantons and half-cantons of the Swiss Confederation.

Of the many countries of federal structure in the present world, few have had a steady enough political form for a long enough while to test their methods of settling controversies between their member states. Two, however, have lived with outstanding success for well over a century under constitutions that entrust this function to their chief organs of general judication. The aim of this book is to compare the operation of these two courts, the Supreme Court of the United States of America and the Federal Tribunal of the Swiss Confederation, in their disposal of hundreds of these conflicts. This survey is presented with the hope that it may increase understanding of the practice of this method of settlement and may yield values to other federacies, especially to those now building their frame of government, and even to nations in their relations with one another.

Since brevity is the spice of wit, I venture to spice nomenclature and spelling with some brevities which I trust will please the reader's palate if he is apprised of them in advance. So the highest Swiss judicial organ (das Bundesgericht, le Tribunal fédéral) is often simply the Tribunal, and the Supreme Court of the United States of America, the Court; the Swiss chief executive organ (der Bundesrat, le Conseil fédéral), which has some judicial powers, the Council; and the Swiss chief legislative organ (die Bundesversammlung, l'Assemblée fédérale), the Assembly.

Where Webster's third edition offers choice of spellings, in general I use the shorter: thus *sovran, tho, thru, hight*. Like *sovran*, I write *foran*, rejecting the spelling *foreign* (a fantastic distortion based on false etymology) for the familiar adjectival terminal *-an* (as in Anglican, Brahman, Lutheran, Mohammedan, Roman). I unscramble a little the frequent American confusion of the prefixes *for-* and *fore-*, distinguishing *forbear* and *forgo* (expressing restraint) from *forebear* and *forego* (expressing priority). Switzerland being a word as bizarre as would be Italianland, Swits seems to me the proper English equivalent of die Schweiz, la Suisse; but I forgo use of this and several other shortenings that bedecked—or, if you prefer, besmirched—my earlier book, *Law among States in Federacy*, a survey of Swiss intercantonal decisions.

The Constitution of the Swiss Confederation [Art. 116] declares since 1938 that Helvetia has four national languages. So each of the "twenty-two cantons"—that is, nineteen cantons and six half-cantons—may respond to four names. While in English there is some tendency to employ French names even in referring to German-speaking areas (e.g., Bâle or Basle, Berne, Grisons, Lucerne), I speak of each city and canton in the language there prevalent. Thus I use the German name—therefore Basel, Bern, Graubünden, Luzern—for all but the southernmost Italian-speaking canton of Ticino and the five westernmost predominantly French-speaking cantons. But, deferring to settled custom, I employ two anglicized names: Geneva (canton and city) rather than Genève, and Zurich (canton and city) rather than Zürich. I style the six half-cantons Inner and Outer Appenzell, Rural and Urban Basel, Nidwalden and Obwalden (together Unterwalden).

The custom of Swiss legal writers is rarely to mention the names of litigants in referring to decisions of courts, and to designate those of the Tribunal solely by volume, part, and page of its official Reports, Volume I being that for 1875, and one volume—in recent years in four parts—appearing each succeeding year. However, I have followed the Anglo-American practice of entitling Swiss as well as American cases by the names of the parties, the protagonists of these battles of the courthouse.

I am beholden to many who have prepared the way for this study. Half a century ago the Supreme Court's pronouncements in cases between states were carefully assembled by James Brown Scott in *The Judicial Settlement of Controversies between States of the American Union* (1919), and its record was briefly and ably reviewed soon after by Charles Warren in *The Supreme Court and Sovereign States* (1924). Many others have spoken in articles less detailed if not less distinguished. Corresponding writings about the Federal Tribunal are few. The only specific studies are those by Arnold Bolle, *Das Interkantonale Recht* (1907) and by Margrit Gut, *Staatsrechtliche Streitigkeiten zwischen den Kantonen und ihre Beilegung* (1942), both doctoral dissertations at Zurich University, and the book already mentioned, *Law among States in Federacy* (1959). In periodical literature I have found only two articles focused on intercantonal litigation, and these, tho by Swiss jurists, were published only, I believe, in English: Max Huber, "The Intercantonal Law of Switzerland," *American Journal of International Law*, 3 (1909), 62; and Dietrich Schindler, "The Administration of Justice in the Swiss Federal Court in Intercantonal Disputes," *ibid.*, 15 (1921), 149. Briefer description of this federal function can be found in many treatises on constitutional law, such as that by Zaccaria Giacometti, *Schweizerisches Bundesstaatsrecht* (1949). Willard B. Cowles has given us a compared law discussion of a part of this area, with slight attention to Swiss material, in his lectures before the Academy of International Law at The Hague on "International Law as Applied between Subdivisions of Federations," *Recueil des Cours* (1949).

For oral enlightenment also I am grateful to several of the above persons and to many others on both sides of the Atlantic. With warm appreciation also I acknowledge hospitality afforded me by the libraries and librarians of the Tribunal fédéral in Lausanne, the University of Geneva, the United Nations in Geneva, the law schools of Chicago, Harvard, and Yale universities, and the Library of Congress.

CONTENTS

INTRODUCTION

THO I shall of course say much about rules of substantive law, the main intent of this book is not to explore in depth the substantive rules discovered or expounded and used in settling disputes before the Swiss and American courts, but to show to the citizen reader the function of each court in relations between the constituent states of each country. Besides such incidental discussion of substantive rules, our central theme requires that we understand something, and some differences, of judicial procedure. So—but without going into the methods used for gathering and presenting evidence—here at the start and in as nontechnical language as possible, let us take a short look first at the methods of decision of the Federal Tribunal of Switzerland and the Supreme Court of the United States and second at the methods of informing the public of how particular controversies have been terminated.

In cases before the older, the American, court, as most English-reading persons are probably aware, the attorneys of suitors present to the Court and to each other, some days in advance of the time set by the Court for the public hearing of the case, written—or rather printed—arguments and citations of "authority," chiefly judicial precedent ("briefs," they are called, tho frequently very long). Nearly always also at an appointed hour and within a strictly rationed span of minutes, one or more attorneys for each party discusses this material ("argues," not pleads) at a public sitting of the full court, and the justices individually may, and often do, press him with searching oral questions of fact and law.

After this public hearing of arguments before the full bench, the justices retire to consult in closest secrecy and eventually announce an order (in American English, usually called a "judgment") disposing of the case, often accompanied by a common opinion or several opinions (in British English, "judgments"), expressing the Court's grounds for its conclusion. All these judicial pronouncements are written by individual justices and in effect signed by them. Published by the government, in volumes entitled *Cases Adjudged in the Supreme Court* (usually three volumes annually), they are commonly called *United States Reports*. All opinions are published in full. The same opinions appear also in two equally complete and reliable unofficial series: *United States Reports, Lawyers' Edition* (Lawyers Cooperative Publishing Co.); and *Supreme Court Reporter* (West Publishing Co.). The editors of each of the three series summarize prevailing views in extensive "headnotes" preceding the report of each case. Appendix 3 at the end of this book, listing Supreme Court cases mentioned herein, gives citations to the three series.

As for the Swiss Federal Tribunal, its decisions are listed likewise (Appendix 4) with citations to the official reporter, *Entscheidungen des schweizerischen Bundesgerichts, Arrêts du Tribunal fédéral suisse* (one annual volume in four parts, usually bound in two or more books); also to the *Journal des Tribunaux,* a semimonthly periodical which publishes in extenso or in summary very dependable French versions of the more important decisions pronounced in German and Italian. The headnotes in these Swiss reports are keys to, but not summaries of, the decisions.

Because of the several Swiss languages, official publications may be either in one language, in which case there are usually three editions—French, German, and Italian (the Swiss Constitution designates Romansch a "national," but not an "official" language)—or in these three languages intermingled. Of the latter type are the reports of the Tribunal's decisions. Standing rules of the Tribunal determine which of the three official languages shall be used in each decision: in cases appealed from cantonal courts, it is usually the language of the trial; in cases originating in the Tribunal, usually the language of the defendant.

A clerk (Gerichtsschreiber, greffier) versed in the language prescribed for the particular case, not a judge, writes the opinion of the Tribunal. He does this on the basis of a public oral consultation of the "court" or "chamber" of judges assigned to the case. Here the three to seven judges (having previously more or less fully examined the briefs and listened to never interrupted oral arguments, if any) hear a full report of the case by one judge assigned to prepare it; then each other judge orally presents his view, in French or in German, as he prefers, on the disposition of the case. After this *public* consultation, and a *public* vote, the clerk prepares the reasoned judgment or opinion, representing the views of the majority of the court. In the reports of decisions there is never any notation of dissenting views or dissenting judges; these always anonymous decisions perpetuate only the prevailing consensus.

Few (about one in ten) of them are published officially. Occasionally an "unpublished" opinion of the Federal Tribunal appears unofficially in a legal periodical. But the great majority of opinions, those that the Tribunal does not select for publication, can be found only in the archives of the Tribunal. Yet the Tribunal, which has them at hand, often cites them as precedents. This incompleteness of publication appears to be due to frugality in financial outlay of a small country rather than to desire to secrete the Tribunal's performance.

The Tribunal's published (and occasionally unpublished) decisions are subjected to examination and criticism in numerous legal periodicals. But much the greater part—presumably the part that is thought less significant for Swiss readers—of the Tribunal's product has no wide-range law-molding influence, being soon buried in the archives of the

Tribunal beyond recall except by the searcher. I have only nibbled at this mass of dormant material, which includes many intercantonal cases.

Some intercantonal disputes, by choice of the parties or by law of the land, go for settlement to others than the Tribunal; that is, to the Federal Council, the Assembly, ad hoc arbitral boards, or single arbitrators. These also are litigious settlements; but not always settlements by general law, the Council (the plural executive, roughly corresponding to the President of the United States) and the Assembly (established by the Constitution of 1848 on the pattern of the United States Senate and House of Representatives) being primarily political organs. These relatively unusual, generally unpublished, and less strictly law-made and law-making decisions are not examined in this book.

Unless otherwise indicated, all Swiss cases to which reference is made herein are decisions of the Federal Tribunal; all American cases, decisions of the Supreme Court. The study ends with the year 1965 except that Supreme Court cases to the end of the 1965 term (June 1966) are included.

The Tribunal (twenty-six judges and twelve alternates), having a bench thrice as numerous as that of the Court (nine judges), sits for adjudication always in chambers specializing in particular branches of the law. George A. Codding, Jr., in his excellent little book *The Federal Government of Switzerland* (1961) gives a very clear summary of the organization and operation of the Tribunal. It currently disposes of approximately the same number of cases as its American counterpart. The latter delivers full opinions in only about 5 percent of its cases and disposes of another 10 percent on the merits by summary ("per curiam") opinions. The remaining 85 percent are cases that are rejected without consideration of the merits of the controversy as not rating such consideration by the Court, most of them being denials of petitions for review of a lower court's decision ("denial of certiorari"), where the statutes grant the Court this option. Few, if any, cases before the Swiss Tribunal correspond to those in this 85 percent category. For every Swiss decision is disposed of by a single reasoned opinion, written by one of the college of scribes. The average length of the opinion is less than that of a Supreme Court justice's opinion.

The proportion of cases between cantons to all cases before the Tribunal, tho very small, is much larger than the proportion of cases between states to all cases before the Supreme Court. Over the years, this number in each country runs below 1 percent of all cases decided by the respective courts; in the toll of published decisions since 1874, intercantonal cases clearly outnumber American interstate cases disposed of by full opinions, tho Appendix 3 is longer than Appendix 4.

A TALE OF TWO COURTS

1 DRAMATIS PERSONAE
THE CENTER
AND THE COMPONENT
STATES

THE combining into a political entity of previously separate political units without the extinction or devitalization of these units, presents a problem of apportionment of authority between the new central state and the continuing constituent states, cantons, provinces, or units by whatever name they may be known. This division of power between center and component states that is federalism is considered a cornerstone of political liberty in both the Swiss Confederation and the United States. The "separation of powers," legislative, judicial, and executive, also characterizes both countries. In the Swiss structure, the legislative (Federal Assembly) is more potent with respect to the judicial than in the United States; and the executive (Federal Council), collegial and elected for a term of years (like the Federal Tribunal) by the legislative, has been less dominant than is the independently elected President in the United States.

The importance of the Council is clearly increasing, partly because the action and inaction of the Federal Assembly (the Council of States and the National Assembly) are subject to popular control by the initiative and the referendum, used not only mandatorily for constitutional amendments, but also, upon voters' demand, for all legislation and treaties. Like the collegial executive, this process of popular (instead of executive) veto of legislation is now characteristic of

Swiss government at both the confederational and the cantonal levels.

This is not the place to make detailed comparison between Swiss and American federalism, but it needs a brief word. The "oath fellowship" of the cantons, until Napoleon's brief imposition of centralized government (1798–1802), developed only minimal national organs—a central authority weaker than that of the United Nations or even the League of Nations—comparable to the United States *before* the Articles of Confederation. Long before the overthrow of Napoleon, federalism was reestablished by Napoleon's Act of Mediation (1802). The Treaty of Alliance, of 1815, between the cantons set up a regime roughly comparable to that of the United States under those Articles (1781–1789), with a central legislature of very limited powers, a nominal executive (a canton), and no trace of a separate judicial organ. The United States barely survived till the Constitution of 1787 took effect in 1789, and for Helvetia the comparable period of thirty-three years ended in a very brief civil war (1847). This last Swiss war, domestic or foran, was promptly followed by the drafting and adoption of the Constitution of 1848. It was revised thruout (and its articles renumbered) in 1874, and has been amended piecemeal again and again. By this present Constitution the executive (Federal Council) and judicial (a single court, the Federal Tribunal) organs gained independent status. Bern in 1848 became the permanent political capital, and Lausanne in 1875 the seat of the Tribunal. In the terminology of political scientists, a confederation has become a federation. But the name of Confédération Suisse (Schweizerische Eidgenossenschaft) has not been changed.

The biggest formal change in the Constitution of the United States also was made in the aftermath of civil war. While the "Civil War amendments" did not change the well-established frame of national government, they—especially the Fourteenth Amendment (1868) as judicially applied over the succeeding years—greatly limited state powers and both directly and indirectly enlarged those of Congress and the national judiciary. The United States in 1868 and Switzerland in 1875 reached approximately the same degree of centralization and have proceeded in this respect in roughly parallel course since that time.

From the point of view of inquirers about our aspect of federalism, the fact that one country became a giant and the other, in population and area, remained a pigmy, has little significance. The Swiss scheme of government has much greater similarity to that of the United States than it has to that of any other European or Asian country. It may be fairly said that a century ago these two countries were the only republics (except for some turbulent adolescents in Spanish America), larger than a city-state, in the whole world.

Upon the formation of a federacy the central authority is, in the international sense, the state (or at least it is internationally the spokesman of the federal state), and the constituent units wither as persons in international law and politics, tho some residual power of international intercourse may persist in them. Thus, the United States Constitution [Art. 1, sec. 10] prohibits the constituent states, without the consent of Congress, from entering into any agreement or compact of a political nature with any foran power. This is not quite the same as saying that the constituent states can't enter into foran treaties; but, practically, in the United States, the power became defunct, even as to treaties between states and Indian tribes. The Swiss Constitution [Art. 9] affirmatively allows cantons to make foran treaties in a limited field so long as these treaties do not trench upon the rights of other cantons or conflict with the Constitution. And this power is not quite extinct. All foran relations are carried on thru the Federal Council except that direct correspondence with "inferior authorities" in foran states about the subjects mentioned in Article 9 may be carried on by the cantons [Swiss Const. Art. 10].

In the United States [U.S. Const. Art. 1, sec. 10] under the same limitations as apply to the states' foran treaty-making power, and in Switzerland [Swiss Const. Art. 7] under similar ones, constituent states may treat with each other. Thus settlement of interstate disputes may be effected by "compacts" (the usual American term) or "concordats" (the Swiss term for the same thing) resulting from direct negotiation, which are subject to confirmation by the Congress in the former country. The Swiss law does not require confirmation for validity but allows the "federal authority" to prohibit performance of concordats if it would be disruptive. In both countries this internal treaty-making power is far from defunct.

In the distribution of power in the two federacies between the center and the component units the latter are left with a wide area of action—an area in which conflicts may arise between them. These of course may be settled by treaty (compact, concordat) and often are. Indeed in both countries the center has long promoted such agreements as a desirable method of settlement. But the goal is elusive. What if the states do not agree? No settlement and growing tension? Civil war? Defederation? These are the antitheses of the aim of the federal venture. The only course compatible with it is settlement by superior authority.

What national organ should have this settlement function? In a state where federalism is little more than a façade to cover unitary government (Mexico, the Soviet Union, for examples), the power is lodged in the executive or perhaps shared by it with the legislative organ. But where central power is sharply limited, political organs are not authorized to act in all fields where interstate controversy may arise. This is notably true in Canada and Australia. It is only a little less so in the United States, where national legislative power, broad tho it is, is limited to listed subjects and does not include general competence to settle interstate disputes. The Swiss Constitution [Art. 16, and Art. 102, heading 2] authorizes the Federal Council to supervise and curb cantonal difficulties not subject to judicial control. The federal political organs thus may go a long way in ending intercantonal disputes; and the national legislature can and sometimes does expressly give exclusive power over some area to another organ [e.g., Swiss Const. Art. 114 bis]. But in both countries, as well as in Canada, in Australia, and potentially in some other federacies, an area for judicial settlement is part of the federal scheme.

In the United States, by the Articles of Confederation of 1777 (effective 1781) the Congress was expressly authorized to arbitrate between states. By the Constitution this power was converted into adjudication by the Supreme Court. But it did not prevent a civil war. Under the Swiss frame of government prior to the Constitution, a vaguer power of the Diet (hardly more than a diplomatic conference of cantons) was ineffective to prevent the civil war of 1847. By the Constitution of the next year the power of intercantonal settlement in the area of public law was by implication shared by the Federal Council and the National Assembly till 1875, when the establishment of a Federal Tribunal of full-time judges elected for six-year terms was accomplished by the 1874 general revision of the Constitution. There was an enlargement of the judicial function of the Confederation and the creation of regular judicial process (as contrasted to ad hoc arbitration or settlement by political organs) as the normal channel for the resolution of intercantonal controversies. So today in each country the highest court is the usual forum for settlement of controversies between constituent states, so far as that court esteems them to be legal, rather than political.

What controversies are legal controversies between states that may be taken to the Court or the Tribunal, respectively, for adjudication? How does one recognize a state right or a state obligation? Of course contracts, including treaties, engender legal rights and duties between the contracting parties. And if they are treaties of the type usually called conventions, they may endow individuals also with benefits or burdens and enable them also to sue on such rights and subject them to suit on such duties. In other words, these interstate political contracts may give birth to legal rights and duties both of the contracting states and also of other persons.

Rights and duties of cantons or states may arise from express language not only of treaties but also of constitutions or statutes. Yet none of the many "no state shall's" of the

United States Constitution has in fact been enforced by suit brought by one state against another. Suits by individuals against officers of states abound, and several suits against states that have resisted national laws for racial integration have been started by the United States (with statutory authority) in its district courts, and have been carried thence to the Supreme Court: *United States v. Alabama* (1960), *Alabama v. United States* (1963), *Louisiana v. United States* (1965), *United States v. Mississippi* (1965).

Litigation between such parties is a frequent way of testing the constitutionality of provincial or dominion statutes in Canada, where the case is usually styled Attorney General of Canada v. Attorney General of a province, or vice versa. And it is not unusual in Switzerland, e.g., *Confederation v. Urban Basel* (1939). In Australia, Victoria sued the Commonwealth to invalidate national tax legislation and was highly successful, obtaining in 1957 a decision that overruled an earlier one of the same type.

In the United States likewise a state is a person against whom suit may be brought by a sister state to prevent enforcement of its federally unconstitutional laws that would hurt the plaintiff state [*Pennsylvania v. West Virginia* (1923) (restriction of export of natural gas by West Virginia)]. But cases are few. Suit against the officer entrusted with the execution of a statute, federal or state, is more usual. Rarely, a state brings the suit. A case of this kind is *South Carolina v. Katzenbach* (1966), Katzenbach being then attorney general of the United States. There the state, starting its suit in the Supreme Court, tried and failed, on the merits, to stop enforcement of the national Voting Rights Act of 1965.

There is no theoretical difficulty in finding a state, like an individual, liable for a tort, as for a breach of contract or quasicontract. It is liable for its own conduct and at least for some acts of its officers and employees. Is it also liable for the harmful acts of private persons, whose link with a state is by citizenship, domicil, or presence? Is it liable for not preventing or stopping them? The extent of such liability is not clear, but it has been enforced preventively if such acts are persistent. An example is afforded by litigation between states concerning pollution of interstate rivers in the United States. Somewhat similar was the case successfully brought by the canton of Solothurn, which complained in 1900 of the operation of a rifle range in the canton of Aargau. There was no assertion that the operator, a municipality, was an agent of the defendant canton and that that created its liability; it was the failure of Aargau to abate the persistent hazard to which people in Solothurn were subjected that made Aargau liable.

The aggrieved state may guard its rights of property by suing for compensation for damage to it or for specific redress; and the outer bounds of the concept of property are hazy. Even more hazy are the outer limits of a state's standing as protector of the interests of its citizens or those related to it by domicil or by presence. How far is it parens patriae, to use the term evoked by the Supreme Court? The same sort of question exists in Swiss law, phrased as the distinction between the aggrieved canton's *public* law right and the aggrieved individual's civil (or *private*) law right. In *Ticino v. Graubünden* (1923) the plaintiff canton by a public law action vindicated its tax sovranty against intrusion by the defendant's levy of a tax against a citizen of Ticino. But only the citizen himself by a private or civil law action, the Tribunal said, could recover the payment that Graubünden had already exacted from him. Likewise in (what for convenience may be called) *Zurich v. St. Gallen* (1955), the Wardship Authority of Meilen, a district agency of Zurich, could not get redress for the alleged illegal decision of the Wardship Authority of St. Gallen, an agency of St. Gallen, in dealing with a citizen of Meilen, since he had a private law remedy by appeal to the cantonal courts from that decision. Exactly when public law redress by the canton or its agency is allowed in such situations must be puzzling even to those more skilled than I in the Swiss dichotomy between public law and private law. In *Juzi v. Bern and Schaffhausen* (1948), a public law action, it appears that Juzi, after he had paid to Schaffhausen a tax on his succession to certain property and after Bern had levied but not collected an inheritance tax on him with respect to the same property, brought this action against both cantons. The court found, pursuant to the Swiss rule against double taxation, that Schaffhausen's exaction was unlawful and ordered Schaffhausen to pay Bern to the credit of Juzi.

As will be seen in later chapters, Swiss law recognizes that jurisdictional controversies between cantons, whether directly raised, as in *Ticino v. Graubünden,* or indirectly as by Juzi, are proper subjects of litigation before the Tribunal as intercantonal cases. The initiator may be either a canton or an individual threatened or thwarted by a "conflict of competences." Whoever be the plaintiff, these are reckoned public law controversies between cantons. On the other hand, a right of a canton's citizen or domiciliary against another canton cannot be so absorbed by his canton or its agency as to enable it to obtain redress for breach of that right by the other canton. If it tries to do so and this is deemed the whole basis of action, as in *Zurich v. St. Gallen* (1955), the action will be dismissed; if it is deemed a separable part of the action, as in *Ticino v. Graubünden,* no redress for that part will be given. But what claims will be deemed sufficiently public to warrant relief in the intercantonal action, as in *Juzi,* and what will be thrown out, leaving the individual to pursue his rights by seeking administrative or private law redress thru cantonal channels, is, at least to me, not clear.

An international state's sponsoring capacity is almost infinite. But in a federation the member state does not by diplomacy or by litigation care for its people when they are in other states; for the citizen of the federation has access to courts wherever he may be and does not need his state's or his canton's care. Yet he is frequently protected by his state or canton against effects within this state of acts done outside it, even tho he too can sue the wrongdoers. If the state sues not for damages but for *specific* prevention of a wrong or enforcement of a duty, such as for a boundary determination, an apportionment of flowing water, or a limitation of air or water pollution, redress for the state is the same as that for the individual. Then the question is merely, Is there any reason for the state as well as the individual to be accorded standing to sue when the individual is competent to sue for the same thing? If the remedy sought is *damages*, neither the Swiss nor the American state may recover (as an international state can, in asserting a pecuniary claim against another international state) compensation for the losses of its citizen (or other sort of protégé); to recover money it must, apparently, show a "direct" injury to itself.

While this limitation of a state's right applies to suits against individuals as well as those against other states, the limitation is vitally important when its effect is to bar recovery completely; that is, in legal systems in which states may be sued by other states but may not be sued by individuals. Since this is generally their situation under American law and the Eleventh Amendment to the Constitution confirms this rule, the Supreme Court, for this as well as for other reasons, has repeatedly struggled over the state's standing as parens patriae to sue another state; that is, to sue for redress of harm suffered primarily by its people. Indeed the Supreme Court sets this question off from the question of liability of the party sued, whenever its original jurisdiction is invoked on any score, by conditioning such suits upon its granting an initial motion for permission to sue. So far as I have discovered, neither the Swiss Federal Tribunal nor the courts of other federacies that adjudicate cases between constituent states have developed this practice of initiating suit between states by a "motion for leave to file" the suit.

I have suggested one reason for the American practice, namely, that it is good to determine at the threshold whether the suit is barred by the Eleventh Amendment. Another reason, perhaps, is to limit the quantity or variety of controversies that may be cast into the Court's lap as original jurisdiction cases. At least it is a fact that, tho in the Swiss Confederation political power is no less centralized than in the United

States, the number of cases between the twenty-five cantons and half-cantons is greater than that of cases between the fifty much larger states. And their variety also is greater.

Parens patriae standing in suits against states has often been accorded to a plaintiff state which seeks to protect natural resources for users within the state—water flow since *Kansas v. Colorado* (1902), gas transmission since *Pennsylvania v. West Virginia* (1923), purity of streams since *Missouri v. Illinois* (1901), and, to mention suits not against states, purity of air since *Georgia v. Tennessee Copper Co.* (1907), purity of ocean since *New Jersey v. New York City* (1931). But parens patriae standing is wider; how wide, however, must remain vague when the Court decides contrarily *Oklahoma v. Atchison Ry.* (1911) and *Georgia v. Pennsylvania R.R.* (1945), professing not to overrule the Atchison case.

One of the Court's longer statements concerning the amplitude of the parens doctrine occurs not in an interstate case but in an appellate case, in which a state officer, rather than the state itself, was nominally plaintiff. This is *Hopkins Loan Association v. Cleary* (1935), a case in which the state, in the person of its Banking Commission, succeeded in preventing a change of charter by a banking corporation it had created. "In the creation of corporations of this quasi-public order and in keeping them thereafter within the limits of their charters," the Court said, "the state is parens patriae acting in a spirit of benevolence for the welfare of its citizens." A description of a wide authority indeed. But when it is invoked by one state against another, it sometimes seems to shrink.

The Swiss Tribunal has not used the term parens patriae, but it recognizes the right. Thus one of the reasons for relief in the shooting range case was that Solothurn "has the right and duty to care for the general public safety of the inhabitants of its territory."

Cases between American states remain so few that each one, once it has jumped the first hurdle of leave to file, is tailor-cut and time-consuming. Interstate litigation after a century and three-quarters is still looked upon as exceptional and out of course. But should it be so? Cases of several types between cantons of the Swiss Confederation are routine: suits challenging taxation by another canton of some property or activity taxable assertedly only by the plaintiff canton, controversies about which of two or more cantons may administer an estate or may or must try an accused, or must support an indigent—these questions are normal grain for the Tribunal's mill-wheels of justice. But as issues between states of the North American union, they are unknown to or rejected by the Court, sometimes on the ground of lack of standing of the plaintiff state, sometimes on the ground of nonexclusiveness of state competence. But should not the American Court learn from Swiss experience? This would in a way return the compliment that the Swiss Confederation gave to the United States when it set up in 1848 its parliament of two houses like the Congress of the United States and launched the only European government in which neither the executive nor the legislative branch is accountable to the other, but each, as a separate center of political power, must cooperate with the other and accommodate for the national well-being. But if the Supreme Court has ever alluded to an intercantonal decision of the Federal Tribunal—indeed to any case between states in any foran country—the allusion has escaped me.

References by the Swiss Tribunal to American interstate cases are equally absent. Neither Huber nor Schindler, writing for American readers, mentions any, nor have I found any since their day. But this disregard is less surprising, for the Tribunal's decisions, tho constantly relying on earlier decisions as authority or at least as important justification, are never decorated with footnotes in the style of twentieth-century Supreme Court opinions, nor are they brocaded with the strings of citations of cases that are part of the customary dress of American judicial writing.

Of course the persuasiveness of decisions under the constitutional system of one country is not high in another country with a different, albeit in many ways a similar, constitutional system—not to mention the differences in language and jurisprudential heritage of the two countries with which we are concerned.

How significant in a federacy are suits between its states? Where the state is in general immune from suit, as by the traditional rule of Anglo-American law, it may be thought almost essential to the "rule of law" that states be suable by other states. If every sort of claim against a state were also a claim against some state officer, one state's right to sue another state would perhaps be superfluous. But certain claims against it, most obviously claims for performance of promissory agreements, are not deemed claims against any state officers. So amenability of states to suit by some plaintiff is a necessity if lawful behavior of states is important for the assurance of justice and order between the units of the federacy.

A second value of the Swiss and American regimes of interstate settlement is that they provide a probably dispassionate, because national, adjudicator. With its consent, even in a country that immunizes the state from suit, the state may be sued. But when consent is given, it is ordinarily consent to be sued only in its own court, which may have, or may be suspected to have, some bias. When presented to a federal authority, the claim will be evaluated by probably more competent and impartial judges than if the defendant's forum alone is available. This impartiality is further assured by the Swiss Judicature Act's exclusion, by its Article 22, paragraph 1, heading e, of the judge of the Federal Tribunal from sitting in cases concerning his own town or canton, a rule that causes no difficulty because only a small fraction of the Tribunal's bench sits in any case.

In the International Court of Justice, the risk of bias in favor of one's own land is cured in the opposite way. The Statute of that court, Article 31, says, "Judges of the nationality of each of the parties shall retain their right to sit," but it provides for the addition of a judge chosen by every party state from which there is no regular judge sitting. Such a "national" judge sits only ad hoc, for the particular suit for which he is appointed.

The United States Supreme Court follows neither practice. Nor law nor custom causes a justice to withdraw because his state is a litigant. Yet there is no evidence that state bias has in fact impaired the Court's performance, tho—or perhaps because—its judges, unlike those of the Swiss Federal Tribunal or of the International Court of Justice, are life tenants of their office.

A third advantage of interstate suits is that they provide an excellent means for developing boundaries between states in the execution of their rights and duties as political persons. In Switzerland and Canada and Australia similar suits between the central government and a canton or province frequently settle between them also such ideal boundaries.

What light does the interstate settlement jurisdiction of the high courts of federacies give for the development of patterns of international settlement? It would be at least as desirable that international states should subject themselves to a regime of law, found and applied, in event of dispute, by judicial agencies, as that intrafederate states should do so. This is merely saying that law should replace war as the ultimate arbiter of group disputes. The difficulty is to agree sufficiently on the standards of decision—to make right balance between stability and development; also to agree on who shall make the law and who shall apply it, for "a government of laws," no less than "a government of men," requires men to run it. By a government of laws we mean indeed a government of men, but one in which the governed governors have reached enough consensus to entrust all points of dissensus to selected persons or agencies for settlement, by legislative process or by judicial process—the consensus including agreement on which process for various types of controversies.

The types of settlement, the legislative and the judicial, differ markedly in the magnitude of invention that may be utilized. The work of courts is more precedented, consistent, and cautious than that of parliaments; and it is confined to the orderly and channeled cure of developed conflicts or the orderly and channeled prevention of imminent conflicts, always conflicts between specific persons. Legislators, on the other hand, typically anticipate conflicts, or dispel gathering clouds by statutory fiat made palatable by political skills of invention, rationalization, compromise, dramatization, and sublimation, and ultimately enforced by judgment of supporting courts, with the help of marshalls and sheriffs. To devise judicial organs and procedures and define their realm is easy compared with the problem of devising legislative organs wise enough to anticipate—and enjoying enough public confidence to be able to resolve—the passionate differences of the arms-bearing groups that we know as international states.

Once the form and authority of the legislature, the chief law-changer, is agreed, the problem of courts is simple, whether the state be unitary or federal. But without agreement on an orderly and not too difficult mode of law-change, an agreed substantive law and procedure for its application would prove to be a strait jacket. We cannot expect a powerful international judicial organ until we set up an effective world legislative organ.

For the three reasons that I have mentioned, the "jurisprudence," as the French say—the body of decisions—of the Swiss and American top courts in litigation between the constituent units of the respective federations is enlightening for every emerging federacy and marks a road that international adjudication also may in some respects travel.

It is to this traveled road of adjudication between the component states of these two old federacies and to the differences in its course that we now turn our attention.

2 JUDICIAL JURISDICTION AND STATE IMMUNITY

IN both countries the constitution lays the foundation for judicial dealing with disputes between component states. Article 3 of the older constitution, that of the younger country, from the start (1789) gave the Supreme Court power to decide "controversies between two or more States." The newer constitution, but of the more ancient federacy, at first (Constitution of 1848, Art. 101) cautiously empowered the Federal Tribunal "as a court of civil law" to adjudicate "controversies, provided they do not relate to public law, between cantons," but only if the Federal Council (executive) referred such cases to the Tribunal. It was only after the general constitutional revision of 1874 that the Tribunal was empowered to deal with intercantonal cases of public law nature.

The United States Constitution defines the boundaries of the Supreme Court's *original* jurisdiction (i.e., the power to adjudicate cases, such as these between states, that are started in, not appealed to, the Supreme Court), a jurisdiction that can be neither straitened nor widened by the Congress. But the Swiss Constitution expressly allows the National Assembly to alter the Tribunal's jurisdiction. Moreover it places *federal* statutes and treaties beyond judicial "control" (rejection for unconstitutionality). It is therefore the statutory law, rather than the Constitution, that determines the Tribunal's authority. Hence the Swiss Judicature Act is more authoritative than the United States Judicial Code, to which the Constitution is superior, as was decided in *Marbury v. Madison* (1803).

In the course of years both constitutions have been amended in their definitions of their high courts' power to deal with cases in which states are parties.

The Eleventh Amendment to the United States Constitution (1795) curtailed the general suability of states; but not their suability by other states, or by the United States. Overriding *Chisholm v. Georgia* (1792), the Eleventh Amendment established or confirmed a distinction in the susceptibility of a state of the federation to suit that does not trouble the Swiss courts: the distinction between suit by a plaintiff which is, and suit by a plaintiff which is not, a state of the federation.

It must be acknowledged that the Supreme Court's holding in *Chisholm v. Georgia* that the Constitution authorized individuals to sue states was contrary to contemporary opinions strongly expressed in the debates concerning adoption of the Constitution, and was received with appall by public opinion. It was felt to subordinate the states to the federal judicial power to a degree that subverted the equipoise of federalism. And since at that period probably no state or sovran in the world was subject to suit in any court, it is not surprising that, to overrule *Chisholm v. Georgia*, the Eleventh Amendment was adopted. To narrow the judicial authority of the Supreme Court in some such way was indeed a necessity of practical politics. For suits against states brought by individuals (largely Tory refugees and other aliens, of whom Chisholm was one) were already crowding into the Supreme Court. If they had been entertained, the Court soon would have been overloaded with highly unpopular claims and hampered in performance of its main function of sustaining federal authority against encroachment by the states, or vice versa.

We may regret that the great argument of Edmund Randolph in support of the Court's jurisdiction in *Chisholm v. Georgia* and the able opinions of Chief Justice John Jay and others of the majority perished from the hard blast of the

Eleventh Amendment. This fully restored or, if you agree with the minority in *Chisholm v. Georgia,* confirmed the immunity of states from suit except that they remained suable in the Supreme Court by other states of the federation (and, as the Court later held, by the United States, but not, as the Court decided only in 1934, in *Monaco v. Mississippi,* by a foran state).

So under the national law of the United States, since the Eleventh Amendment, a state, unless consenting to be sued [*Clark v. Barnard* (1883)], is subject to suit only by other states of the Union and by the United States, and by the constituent states only in the Supreme Court of the United States.

However necessary politically was this amendment—or at least some amendment—after the Supreme Court's *Chisholm* decision, it was retrograde action to constitutionalize the immunity of states, itself a reflection of the immunity of the King of England. For such immunity conflicts with the democratic notion that the rule of law, judicially enforced, applies to governments.

While the United States has the same customary immunity as the states, it has consented by statute to be sued in constantly broader areas of liability; while states have been more conservative than the United States in consenting to be sued. Also, suit against public officers, both state and federal, is a means by which persons may obtain extensive specific prevention of, and, more rarely, reparation for, illegal official action. This yields much of what could be obtained by suit against the United States. But boundaries are not clear [*Georgia R.R. and Banking Co. v. Redwine* (1952)]. An outstanding exposition of the complex state of this area of the law was published in Volume 70 (p. 827) of the *Harvard Law Review,* "Remedies against the United States and Its Officials" (1957), and was followed in 1963 by historical and analytical articles by Louis L. Jaffe, "Suits against Governments and Officers" (*HLR,* 77: 1 and 209), which show the irregular currents of the law of sovran immunity in Anglo-American jurisprudence.

Nonsuability of states by other states, except when the defendant consents, is a basic doctrine of international law. But one of the characteristics of federacy, notably of Swiss and American federacy, is adjudication of disputes between the component states on demand of the plaintiff, exposure of each state to suit by any of its peers.

It is noteworthy in this connection that India, a recruit to federalism with dominantly English law background, has diminished (following legislation of the United Kingdom) the general immunity of the state, constituent and central [Const. of India, Arts. 300 and 361]. Regarding suits between these states, the Constitution of India [Art. 131] provides that its Supreme Court shall have original and exclusive jurisdiction of those involving questions of legal rights "(a) between the Government of India and one or more States; (b) between the Government of India and any State or States on one side and one or more other States on the other; or (c) between two or more States" (with certain exceptions).

In the Swiss Constitution of 1874, Article 110, the revision of Article 101 of 1848 (previously quoted), reads: "The Federal Tribunal adjudicates civil law controversies . . . between cantons." There is also Article 113: "The Federal Tribunal adjudicates . . . controversies between cantons of public law nature." These provisions do not lessen state immunity from suit as does the corresponding part of Article 3 of the United States Constitution, for in Swiss law there is no immunity of the state; but like Article 3, they define the jurisdiction or competence of the high court; they name the normal forum in which cantons fight their legal battles with one another.

In the course of years since 1874 "civil law controversies" have ceased to arise between cantons. Perhaps they lurk ghostly in the archives of the Palais du Tribunal in Lausanne, but none has found its way into the published reports since the twentieth century began.

But this is not strange. Under the 1848 Constitution only civil law controversies between cantons, not public law ones, could be settled by the Tribunal. Yet the line between these two types of suit is far from firm. Thus, if cantons make contracts with one another about matters of public concern—road-building, education, conservation—and then disagree as to their meaning, there arises a claim of breach of contract such as might occur between private persons who contract with one another, does it not? Yes, said the court before 1875, it's a civil law controversy between cantons, one that is proper for us. (Perhaps in reality the Tribunal made the opposite approach: It is proper for us since the Federal Council has referred it to us; so we'll consider it a civil law case.) On the other hand it may be argued that these are public treaties between cantons relating to the performance of governmental functions; and therefore claims of breach are *public* law claims. "The difficulty is that a public authority may sometimes undertake the same activity in a public or private law capacity," says Wolfgang Friedmann, writing on "The Changing Functions of Contract in the Common Law," *University of Toronto Law Journal,* 9 (1951), 15. Latterly it is the public law aspect that has dominated the Swiss court's view of such intercantonal litigation, concerning both contracts and property rights. While the difference between public law and civil law is deeply felt in Helvetia, and so is reflected in the Constitution, yet, with the swing of the pendulum toward public law, which Dr. Friedmann lays forth, civil law controversies between cantons have become ghosts. The Swiss judges whom I have asked to explain this desiccation of civil law litigation between cantons have offered nothing more specific than that, to quote a letter from Eugen Blocher, a former president of the Tribunal, "the concept of civil law controversies was formerly expanded to embrace situations which today are rightly considered as of a public law nature." Perhaps the only tenable position is that, in intercantonal litigation, a cleavage between civil and public law is undiscoverable; there is an overlap of the areas. No Swiss jurist discussing intercantonal disputes has succeeded in drawing a fast line.

The fading from the reports of civil law cases between cantons, a trend expressed also in the statutory transfer in

1943 of controversies over cantonal citizenship from the civil law to the public law jurisdiction of the Tribunal [Judicature Act, Art. 83, heading c] does not mean that the Tribunal will allow what it characterizes as private or civil law claims of *individuals* to be settled by public law actions between cantons or their agencies. (Differentiation between suits between cantons, i.e., suits in which usually the parties named are the chief executive organs which are, by the way, always councils of three or more persons, and suits between lesser officers or organs of the opposing cantons, has no significance for us; they both are governed by Article 83 of the Judicature Act. So ordinarily I entitle them all as suits between cantons. In the American law, however, they must be differentiated, for two reasons: first, the state, but not its officers or agencies—unless the Supreme Court assimilates them to the state [*Arkansas v. Texas* (1953)]—may institute actions in the Supreme Court; and second, the immunity or nonsuability of states—with the exception that other states may implead them in the Supreme Court—does not extend to the agencies or officers of states.) The application of the distinction between the private right and the public or state's right is no easier to make in Swiss law than is the parallel distinction in American law between what rights are so personal that the law—and in suits against states, specifically the Eleventh Amendment—forbids a state to sue on them, and what rights, tho personal, are nevertheless also so general that a state may, as a warden of the public welfare, as parens patriae, sue on them. Some cases illustrating this distinction have been already mentioned, and what is said now is far from the last word. This is, and will remain, an area of unpredictability, where judges behind a mask of judicial obligation direct the expansion or contraction of a major function, in these two federal systems, of their august department of national government.

Since all the decisions between cantons that have been reported during the last sixty years have been made not by the civil law chambers of the Tribunal, but by its public law chamber (except for a case now and then in a penal law chamber), the significant provision of the Constitution is Article 113, paragraph 1, heading 2, which, inserted in the revision of 1874 and never altered, gives the Federal Tribunal jurisdiction in "controversies between cantons of public law character."

The present Article 83 of the Judicature Act (otherwise numbered, but textually the same, in the original [1875] and intermediate versions of the Act) repeats this language, but limits it by adding (as it has read since the revision of December 16, 1943): "when a cantonal government presents the matter and it is one which is not within the jurisdiction of the Federal Council by reason of special provisions of federal legislation." Such statutory attribution of jurisdiction to the Council, it should be noted, is expressly authorized for "administrative controversies" [Swiss Const. Art. 113, par. 2].

Before 1875, settlement of public law intercantonal disputes (and civil law cases that the Federal Council refused to refer to the Tribunal) was entrusted by the Constitution to the Federal Assembly, the legislative organ. Today it is the Federal Council that is named as the repository of intercantonal controversy jurisdiction denied to the Tribunal. Whether or not such denying statutes (relating to water power and other specific subjects) are founded on express mandate of the Constitution, the Tribunal respects them, without inquiring whether the controversies covered are "administrative"—whatever that may mean. It must respect them because of the general rule of the third paragraph of Article 113—that the Tribunal is obliged to apply "the laws and general resolutions passed by the Federal Assembly and the treaties which it has ratified"; that is, apply them without inquiring about their conformity with other provisions of the Constitution.

The Constitution expressly authorizes the Federal Assembly not only to restrict, but also [Art. 114] to enlarge the jurisdiction of the Tribunal.

Swiss interstate judicial jurisdiction differs from American, then, in that it may be (and has been) altered by statute. And, pursuant to Article 113, paragraph 3, the Tribunal is bound thereby.

A nicer example than the Swiss of steady movement, in the last century and a half, from diplomatic to legislative to judicial settlement of disputes between states, would be hard to discover. When the Swiss Confederation displaced the Napoleonic Helvetic Republic, the Diet or permanent diplomatic conference of the cantons—the General Assembly, to use the term for the similar organ of the United Nations— was charged with responsibility to keep the peace between them but only by the methods of mediation and voluntary arbitration. The Diet died with the adoption of the Constitution of 1848, which added to settlement by ad hoc arbitration the alternative of settlement by the Federal Assembly, the newly created legislative organ of the union, or, if the executive Federal Council chose, settlement, but only of disputes of "civil law" type, by the new Federal Tribunal. Experience with the work of this agency, manned by part-time judges and having many judicial duties besides the occasional settlement of disputes between cantons, led to its strengthening in 1874. Full-time judges supplanted part-time, and its jurisdiction was greatly enlarged, notably by opening it to all suits between cantons that the Tribunal should find to be legal in character, except those of such sorts as the legislature should entrust to settlement by the executive. In course of time the Tribunal by decision established that it, and not the executive, construed the law defining the exceptional sphere of the executive; and it further asserted in 1952 in the case of *Fribourg v. Federal Council* that even when decision was entrusted to the executive, the decision should be legal rather than political. But the Tribunal does not assert power to review such executive decisions.

During the last ninety years, too, the court has by its decisions transformed into legal issues many that once were political. So that today, tho in the United States discords between states concerning extradition, "double" taxation, and support of indigent migrants are political matters—matters for negotiation between states—in Switzerland, with some encouragement from their mention in the Constitution, they as a class (but always subject to overruling by federal legislation) are subject to settlement by suit between cantons.

The growth of *judicial* prohibition of taxation of the same object by more than one canton springing from the constitutional command [Art. 46] introduced in 1874, that the Federal Assembly should enact *legislation* to assure this, which it has never done, has been paralleled by a like development from constitutional and statutory texts by layer upon layer of court decisions, of a complex law which enables one canton to recover from another the cost of poor relief which it has given to the latter's indigent citizens in permanent need. This giant of Swiss interstate litigation has one leg planted in the constitutional right of the citizen of any canton to live in any other so long as he does not become a *permanent* charge [Swiss Const. Art. 45] and the other leg in the private law right of a person who performs another's neglected duty to be repaid by him for what is sometimes called in Anglo-American law the latter's "unjust enrichment" [*Urban Basel v. Solothurn* (1882)]. The duty to repay has in course of time grown to include kinds of claims formerly deemed political. Thus, when Geneva asked Bern to reimburse its outlay for indigent Bernese sent home from France who were so ill that, on their arrival at the Swiss frontier, Geneva hospitalized them till they were able to travel farther, or sometimes buried them, and when Bern refused because they were not shown to be persons in *permanent* need, Geneva petitioned the Federal Council to provide some alleviation of this recurrent burden of caring for such "confederals" (citizens of other cantons) arriving from abroad in temporary distress. The Council recommended resort to the Tribunal, which, thus encouraged, responded to Geneva's suit against Bern by allowing recovery, despite the temporariness of the travelers' need, because this need had developed outside the Federation [*Geneva v. Bern* (1924)]. A similar mutation of a claim from the political or moral to the legal realm occurred when the court decided that when public assistance is furnished by canton A to a person in permanent need who is a citizen of both A and B, canton B is liable to canton A for half the cost [*Luzern v. Neuchâtel* (1947), *Urban Basel v. Fribourg* (1951)]. Previously the court had repeatedly declared that such liability for contribution did not exist except when cantons had agreed to it by intercantonal compact.

So "when a cantonal government presents the matter," the Tribunal's door is always open. If the canton fails to prevail, its failure is not for lack of right to enter, but for lack of legal merit in the claim it asserts. The bringing of a case to the court is ipso facto the *assertion* of a legal right. But if a canton cannot persuade the court that it has such a right against the defendant, then judgment goes to the defendant on the merits.

Unlike the Swiss canton, the state, in form at least, has first to push aside the barrier of Rule 5 of the Supreme Court's Rules of Procedure, which requires a would-be plaintiff state to move for "leave to file" suit. On this motion the Court inquires as to the state's standing to bring the action [*Georgia v. Pennsylvania R.R.* (1945), *Arkansas v. Texas* (1953)]. As the Supreme Court expressed this limitation in *Massachusetts v. Mellon* (1923), the effect of Article 3, section 2 of the Constitution "is not to confer jurisdiction upon the Court merely because a State is a party, but only where it is a party to a proceeding of judicial cognizance."

In contrast to the American Constitution, which is construed to allow the United States to sue a state, but not vice versa, the Swiss Constitution, which empowers the Tribunal to decide [Art. 110] "civil law controversies between the Confederation and the cantons" and [Art. 113] "conflicts of competence between federal authorities on one side and cantonal authorities on the other" (which seems to be equivalent to public law controversies between the Confederation and a canton), and the Judicature Act [Arts. 41 and 86] embody the principle of litigative reciprocity between canton and Confederation. The somewhat similar language of the two constitutions is construed quite differently. That the Tribunal decides suits between the Confederation and a canton means that a canton can sue the Bund, as well as vice versa, while the corresponding phrases [U.S. Const. Art. 3] empowering courts of the United States to settle "Controversies to which the United States shall be a Party" (construed to include suits of the Union *against* a state) and giving to the Supreme Court original jurisdiction over "all suits" under Article 3 in which "a State shall be Party," do not enable a state, by virtue of being a state, to sue the nation. To be sure, this conclusion has negative support from the omission of mention of the United States in the bestowal of jurisdiction on courts of the United States to decide "Controversies between two or more States," the phrase which has been construed to abolish at the same time the sovran immunity from suit (by another state) of constituent states of the Union.

The question of standing to sue is not peculiar to states as suitors. That a person has done wrong does not mean that the person who chooses to sue him wins, for this suitor may not be a person of the sort recognized to be victims of the wrong. Courts often do not separate this element of a claim from other elements. But, as has been said, the Supreme Court does when a state wants to bring suit. I have contributed to *Perspectives of Law* (honoring Austin Wakeman Scott, 1964) an essay on the standing of states to invoke the Supreme Court's original jurisdiction; and the general Anglo-American law concept of standing to sue has been ably explored by several scholars, recently and notably by Professor Louis L. Jaffe, in "Standing to Secure Judicial Review," *Harvard Law Review*, 74 (1961), 1265, and 75 (1961), 255. The Swiss court has never separated this issue from the general consideration of the merits of intercantonal claims.

This procedural difference of the treatment of standing by the two courts is not momentous. But the substantive difference in the suability of the center—the Swiss Confederation, the United States—is a matter about which a word more should be said before entering upon an examination of the subject matter of disputes that are litigated between constituent states.

While the United States is by statute now suable by states, as well as by other persons, on claims of many types, there is still no general consent of the United States to be sued by states, and, so far as it has consented, the claim of a state, like that of any other suitor, may be asserted only in the Court of Claims or other inferior court in which the statute permits the litigation; for, as the Supreme Court said in *Minnesota v. United States* (1939), "it rests with Congress to determine not only whether the United States may be sued, but in what court the suit may be brought." Against this defendant neither the Constitution nor any statute gives states the right to bring action in the Supreme Court.

But tho the front door of no court is open to the suer of the United States except to the extent that federal statutes allow, and tho that of the Supreme Court is not open at all (except in its exercise of review of lower court decisions), states in substance may participate in litigation questioning the conduct of the United States. A state, like an individual, may sue an officer of the United States; and, in the more frequent situation of an individual's suit, states, if the matter is one of wide importance, may seek and usually obtain leave of court to present briefs (or, rarely, oral arguments) as "friends of the court." Indeed by this device a suit by or against an individual may in effect be taken over by the state or by the United States more or less as a substitute for that individual.

Thus *Baker v. Carr* (1962) was started in a district court of the United States by some Tennessee voters to compel state election officers to halt the existing method of electing members of the state legislature, which, the plaintiffs said, denied them "equal protection of the laws." When this case reached the United States Supreme Court, where it was thrice argued, among the protagonists were the Attorney General of Tennessee (one of the defendants), the Governor of Oklahoma (as amicus curiae), and the United States by its Solicitor General Archibald Cox, who, "by special leave of the Court, reargued the case for the United States, as amicus curiae," successfully supporting the demand of the original plaintiffs. Two years later when the parallel case concerning representation in the United States House of Representatives, *Wesberry v. Sanders* (the Governor of Georgia) and others, was carried up to the Supreme Court, the United States, by leave, presented brief and argument in successful support of the demand of the plaintiffs, who were voters of Georgia. Meanwhile the Maryland Committee for Fair Representation, a group of voters, had sued the governor (Tawes) and other officers of Maryland and ultimately won from the Supreme Court similar redress (1964). Before that body Solicitor General Cox again appeared for the United States as amicus in this and several similar contemporaneous cases. Also the Court accepted amical briefs from Arizona, Hawaii, Indiana, Kansas, Louisiana, New Jersey, North Carolina, North Dakota, Pennsylvania, Rhode Island, South Dakota, Vermont, as well as from the American Jewish Congress, and the president and board of aldermen of Louisville, Kentucky. In these examples the suits were brought against officers of several states and the United States played a major role on behalf of the plaintiffs. But the privilege of amical participation by states is granted likewise in actions against federal officers and agencies. Thus in *South Carolina v. Katzenbach* (1966), the unsuccessful suit in which South Carolina sought to compel the attorney general of the United States to refrain from enforcing the Voting Rights Act of 1965, amicus curiae briefs were accepted from many other states and a few of them were allowed to make oral argument—some supporting each of the parties. Moreover when enforcement of a state or national law is primarily the responsibility of some officer or agency other than the attorney general (Department of Justice), suits to prevent its enforcement—as well as suits to enforce it—are usually in fact carried on for the defendant, or the plaintiff, by that department of legal service, and of course at public expense. So the United States or the state, as the case may be, whether or not it is the (or a) nominal party, is in actuality the litigant, despite any theoretical nonsuability of states.

The immunity from suit of the United States (except as it by statute consents to be sued) and (with like exception more limitedly accorded) the immunity of states of the Union from suit, save by the United States or a sister state, is mellowed, but not destroyed, by these practices. So far as it continues, a relic of personal majesty beyond reach of courts, Swiss experience shows that it could well be wiped out.

3 THE RANGE OF CONTROVERSY
IN ADJUDICATION BETWEEN CANTONS
AND BETWEEN STATES
THE "POLITICAL" ISSUE LIMITATION

IT is already clear that the subjects involved in cases of state suing state and of canton suing canton differ in the two countries. We may well take a bird's eye survey of the topography of litigation and define its outer boundaries.

American states have, in the great majority of successful suits, laid claim to territory—political control of certain space and of the people and resources therein. Issues of this kind may arise also between the United States and a state [*United States v. Texas* (1892 and 1896), *United States v. Utah* (1931)]. Tho suits between states on less concrete aspects of "sovranty" have been brought, they are few in the United States, and fewer have succeeded, because the state has not been recognized as having interests of many sorts which it may vindicate by suit against other states. But it is otherwise in Switzerland [*Rural Basel v. Urban Basel* (1937), *Geneva v. Confederation* (1955)].

In both countries, of course, disputes that engage states (and might be recognized as appropriate subjects of suit between them) may be settled also by litigation between private persons—like the river flow case of *Hinderlider v. LaPlata Ditch Co.* (1938)—or between a private person and a state officer (a taxpayer, for example, on one side, and a tax department on the other). Thus any list of cases in which states have appeared as litigants will be far shorter than one of cases raising issues that are in substance legal conflicts between states.

CONFLICTS CONCERNING JURISDICTION

Swiss law tends to treat certain types of conflicts as demanding a decision for one and against the other state. American law is more tolerant of multiplicity in authority to tax, to administer, or to prosecute, and is more apt to base a state's exclusive or superior right or responsibility on a "first to act" rule; so that jurisdiction often overlaps between state and nation, between state and state, and between military and civil establishments—sometimes resulting in complex problems of double jeopardy, such as came to the Supreme Court in a drove in its 1957 term. Such concurrence of power rather offends Swiss legal principles. Thus one canton often sues another to determine which of them is empowered to tax, to try, to administer an estate, or to exercise custody over a person or a person's property, who or which, it is assumed, can be subject to such control by the executive or judicial organs of only one canton. Conflict of jurisdiction between cantons may be positive, as in the tax situation; or it may be negative, that is, all cantons disclaiming responsibility for performance of a public duty which admittedly is that of some canton. A large group of intercantonal cases deals with these "conflicts of competences." This is a term not familiar to American ears, and, except for boundary cases, it is a type of dispute rare in litigation between states.

But it existed in Swiss law before there were statutes (i.e., declaring a person to have but one domicil or setting a single locus of trial for a criminal act) to fortify it. It is not hard to describe a big majority of intercantonal cases as competence-conflicts. Many at the same time are quasicontractual reimbursement actions; that is, ones in which the court decides which canton is to bear the ultimate burden of providing relief for some needy person.

The Swiss emphasis on competence-conflicts produces frequent suits in alternative form. Thus taxpayer X may seek a judicial declaration whether it is to canton A or to canton B that he owes a certain tax, as in *Gut v. Luzern and Nidwalden* (1955); or sue for adjustment between cantons if he has paid the wrong one, as in *Juzi v. Bern and Schaffhausen* (1948). Or one canton may sue others alternatively for costs of care of an indigent whose "home" or whose place of incapacitation is disputed, as in *Luzern v. Zug and Geneva* (1945), and in *Urban Basel v. Solothurn and Rural Basel* (1952). Or (the prosecutor of) one canton may sue (those of) others to determine which has the duty of prosecuting a particular person for an act penalized by federal statute (the enforcement of which rests with cantonal prosecutors), as in *Aargau v. Thurgau and Appenzell* (1950). Whether the competence-conflict between cantons is positive (the tax cases) or negative (the poor-relief cases), a canton or an individual may be the plaintiff.

Tho the Supreme Court granted relief in one such case, *Texas v. Florida* (1939), the substantive law which it has laid down makes it unlikely that the Court will be active in this area [*Massachusetts v. Missouri* (1939)]. This substantive law will be discussed later. Here we need to note that it blocks suits by a state against other states; and no less suits by individuals. For neither the nonsuability of *states* by individuals under state law nor the barrier of the Eleventh Amendment would hinder the individual from success in suing *tax departments* of different states, if the American substantive law saw a conflict of competences, as the Swiss law does, to justify this intercantonal "interpleader" type of action.

Whoever the plaintiff, either or both of two kinds of issues may be presented. The issue may be, What is the criterion for determining which of the cantons is competent?—Is it the *place of occurrence* of some act or event; is it the *allegiance* (cantonality) of some person; is it his *domicil;* or is it some other *attachment* to the canton of the person or thing involved? Or the issue may be, Which of the cantons qualifies with respect to an undisputed criterion?—Did the act or event occur in canton A or canton B; is the indigent a Bernese or a Genevese (or perhaps both); when a person living in Luzern entered a Zurich hospital, did he or did he not move his abode from Luzern to Zurich; did an unmarried physician, a citizen of Neuchâtel, keep or lose his residence in Geneva (that of his parents) while engaged in tours of medical service in Asia?

The Swiss inclination to treat conflicts in terms of state competence extends to conflicts between the Confederation and cantons. A strong instance of the Tribunal's reaching out to fit the circumstances into such a conflict mold is furnished by *Confederation v. Zurich,* an unreported case decided May 24, 1965, where the Tribunal resolved a controversy over the respective authority of the Federal Council and the Zurich commercial court to determine the credit to be allowed a tenant for remodeling a building under a federal law regulating rents. The precise question was whether the federal law which was admitted to govern "should be applied by civil courts [of the canton] or administration agencies" of the Confederation, each of which was refusing to act as the agency of first instance. The Federal Tribunal decided, with stated hesitation, to treat this Alphonse and Gaston situation of reciprocal abstention as a negative conflict, under Article 83, heading a, of the Judicature Act (conflicts of competence between federal and cantonal authorities). Thereupon it resolved it against the Council's position; that is, decided that the Council was the agency to settle the issue between the landlord and the tenant.

But these are not the only sorts of conflicts. Others involve the application of agreed peculiar divisions of political power between cantons. This power is not always divided only vertically, so to speak; the boundary may be more complex. One state may exercise public law rights in the same space as another, may act governmentally beyond its general geographical boundaries. Whether a "servitude," as this is called, exists and what its limits are, are questions that the Swiss Tribunal has adjudicated in controversies between cantons.

The Federal Tribunal has rendered three elaborate decisions involving such public law servitudes of medieval origin, two of them entitled in the name of cantons and the most recent started by a citizen of Thurgau (supported, as the court said, by the cantonal executive of Thurgau) against an organ of the canton of St. Gallen. These cases define the respective rights of two cantons where sovranty in territory is divided [*Luzern v. Aargau* (1882), *Thurgau v. St. Gallen* (1928), *Odermatt v. (Catholic Tax Authority of) St. Gallen* (1943)]. Servitudes of a less important character have been litigated between Schwyz and Uri (1908; 1915; 1951). The two St. Gallen cases are decisions, little affected by federal statutes, concerning a tax levied by an established church (i.e., one performing functions for and supported by a canton) on persons domiciled within the general territorial jurisdiction (political boundaries) of another canton.

In American litigation there is no match for cases of this type. Yet other divisions of the usual bundle of governmental functions are found in diplomatic and military "extraterritoriality" by custom or by treaty, such as the American status of forces conventions, and the immunity and authority accorded to governmental international organizations (states of a sort), such as the United Nations. Also resembling the Swiss cases mentioned are American cases concerning federal enclaves (none of them, I believe, suits in which states are parties), and litigation about concurrent rights in water areas, such as *Nielsen v. Oregon* (1909) and *United States v. California* (1947).

Competence conflicts of the most usual type, that is, boundary disputes, have produced abundant cases in both countries. In a federation consisting of twenty-five instead of fifty units and having far shorter boundary milage per unit and a far longer legal history, boundary disputes, since the Tribunal came into being, have been fewer than west of the Atlantic. The last reported case of this sort was decided in 1907, *Zurich v. Schaffhausen*, a river boundary dispute. A lake boundary dispute, underlying but not adjudicated in *Luzern v. Nidwalden* (1927), was afterwards brought to the Tribunal, which, then and still without complete success, has sought to settle it by mediation, as Dr. Karl H. Spillmann reports in his doctoral dissertation (Zurich, 1954), *Die Kan-*

tonsgrenze mit besonderer Berücksichtigung ihrer Verlegung,
page 121. Altogether, he says, six boundary cases have been
before the Tribunal. Two disputes over mountain peak
boundaries, *Graubünden v. Ticino* (1892) and *Outer Appenzell v. St. Gallen* (1895), and two over frontiers in the Rhine,
both between Schaffhausen and Zurich (1897 and 1907),
involved examination of ancient documents and subsequent
conduct of the adjoining cantons and application of general
principles of international law. Dr. Dietrich Schindler de-
scribes them at some length in the article I cited in my
Preface. To these four, Spillmann's count adds the above-
mentioned pending case of the Lake of the Four Forest Cantons, and an unreported decision (1901) between Zug and
Schwyz. This last, quite different from the others, was a
controversy over which canton was entitled to tax a structure
straddling an undisputed boundary. Eschewing a judgment
of Solomon, the court held that since the greater part of the
herdsman's hut lay in Schwyz, Schwyz was authorized to tax
it all. This may be called a temporary servitude.

Also, it may be mentioned, there have been a few settlements of intercantonal boundaries by arbitration. Spillmann
discovered two since 1874, between Luzern and Schwyz in
1924 and between Schwyz and Uri in 1936. By agreement
between the cantons, in each case a board of three was
appointed, one appointment by each canton and one by the
Confederation; in the former case, the decision was based on
laws; in the latter, by agreement of the parties, on a more
subjective appraisal that may be called equity or political
convenience.

In the United States, the two tax cases already noted and
boundary disputes have been till recently the only conflicts of
jurisdiction settled by suit between states. But the book is not
closed. We now have a recruit, an interstate case concerning
escheat of intangible personal property (business credits),
Texas v. New Jersey, which was adjudicated in 1965 in favor
of the state of the creditor's last known address.

Boundaries have been the subject of most interstate litigation in the United States. Many boundary cases figure large

in political history, and *Rhode Island v. Massachusetts* (1838) was crucial in the development of the Court's original jurisdiction.

Other types of cases are (1) those concerning constitutional and statutory duties of interstate collaboration in judicial or executive administration, (2) claims for breach of formal compacts between cantons or states, and (3) claims for breach of general interstate duties, tort claims.

COOPERATION BETWEEN STATES: WHAT IS POLITICAL?

The cases turning on express constitutional or statutory duties of cooperation are chiefly Swiss. But it was this sort of claim that was decided against Kentucky when, for the first time in the history of litigation between states of the Union, the Supreme Court in 1861 settled a controversy over a matter other than territorial jurisdiction.

In *Kentucky v. Dennison, Governor of Ohio* (1861), the plaintiff had sued to compel the defendant to return a fugitive, "Willis Lago, a free man of color," for trial on the charge that in Kentucky, where slavery was lawful, he "did seduce and entice Charlotte, a slave, . . . to leave her owner and possessor and did aid and assist said slave in an attempt to make her escape."

The governor, rather than Ohio, itself, was named defendant probably because the demand was asserted under a federal statute which provided that "It shall be the duty of the executive authority of the state or territory . . . to cause the fugitive to be delivered." The United States Constitution itself (Art. 4, sec. 2) puts the duty in the passive voice: "A person charged in any state with . . . crime, who shall flee from justice and be found in another state, shall on demand of the executive authority of the state from which he fled be delivered up."

Many Swiss instances may be found of the naming of cantonal officers (but always by the name of the office and not by personal name) as parties in cases where, one may fairly say, the parties are really the cantons themselves. This practice is attributable often to the language of the statute or of the Constitution. For example, Article 45 provides that the decision to deport a citizen of one canton from another canton where he has become a public charge, to his canton of origin, shall be made "by the *government* of his canton of residence, and prior warning thereof shall be sent to the *government* of his canton of origin." The word italicized (by me) means specifically the chief executive authority, which in all cantons is a body of three or more persons.

A close observance of statutory language would require all suits between cantons to be entitled for the *plaintiff* in the name of this organ. For Article 83 of the Judicature Act says that the Federal Tribunal entertains "public law controversies between cantons when a cantonal *government* starts the suit." And this style is often, but not always, used.

Variations of nomenclature in Swiss intercantonal suits seem to have no significance. Nor do I find any in naming Governor Dennison as defendant in the case concerning Lago's extradition; indeed the Court had said in *Governor of Georgia v. Madrazo* (1828), an appellate case: "where the chief magistrate of a State is sued not by his name, but by his style of office, and the claim made upon him is entirely in his official character, we think the State itself may be considered as a party. . . ." (And since this was the only party defendant, the Court dismissed the suit pursuant to the Eleventh Amendment.) Dennison was sued both "by his name" and by "his style of office," and the claim related to his conduct as an officer and agent of Ohio. So, tho this seems to make the case one against Ohio, the Court refused to enforce the duty imposed by the federal Constitution on the state. It talked only of the governor's duty and said that it was political (tho not using this word), that the governor had a duty of "fidelity" to surrender the fugitive, but that the Court would not compel him.

The question of whether a state's duty is legal (judicially enforceable) or only one of "fidelity," morality, political responsibility, had been considered by the Court in *Rhode Island v. Massachusetts* (1837), the first case between states in which it gave a final judgment (1846). The question here

took the slightly different form of whether the dispute between the states over their common boundary presented a
legal or a political issue. To sustain its power to dispose of
Rhode Island's boundary claim the Court referred first to the
preconstitutional Articles of Confederation, which had entrusted to the Congress the settlement of "all disputes and
differences now subsisting or that may hereafter arise between two or more states concerning boundary, jurisdiction,
or any other cause whatever," and found its own authority in
the like entrustment for settlement of "controversies between
two or more states" to the Supreme Court by Article 3 of the
Constitution. For thereby, said the Court, "the question
ceases to be a political one . . . ; it comes to the court to be
decided by its judgment, legal discretion, and solemn consideration of the rules of law appropriate to its nature as a
judicial question. . . . Controversies between states . . . are
in their nature political when the . . . state reserves to itself
the right of deciding on it [*sic*]."

In the next chapter we shall return to this foundation case
of interstate adjudication in the United States. The objection
that boundary controversies are political rather than legal
was again rebuffed in *Florida v. Georgia* (1855) and *Virginia
v. West Virginia* (1870), but has not been heard since. It was
likewise advanced and rejected in the first river-diversion
case, *Kansas v. Colorado* (1902), for, as we shall see, the
Court here was treading an area disputed between law and
politics.

This objection that a question brought to the Court is
political rather than legal has been raised in a wide variety of
cases between individuals as well as states. It had a very
intensive examination recently in *Baker v. Carr* (1962), the
first "one-man-one-vote" case. But this examination hardly
bears on the question of what are, between states, to be
regarded as political issues.

Like the Supreme Court in *Kentucky v. Dennison*—that is,
without ever using the phrase "political question"—Abram
Chayes, former Legal Adviser to the United States Department of State, treats of this limitation of judicial action, in a

1965 article in the *Harvard Law Review,* "A Common Lawyer
Looks at International Law" (vol. 76, p. 1396), as a great but
constantly shifting limitation on judicial settlement of international disputes, and finds both there and in constitutional
adjudication gradual emergence of matters from the political
to the legal—particularly matters of review of legislative
conduct. Thus for a long time the Court refused to undertake
to adjudge the constitutionality of laws relating to political
representation. Then gradually it gave more and more protection to electoral rights. But "only in the last couple of years,"
Chayes writes, "has the evolution proceeded to the point that
the Court was willing to review legislative apportionment.
Baker v. Carr." In the *South West Africa Cases* (1966) this
question was a major matter of disagreement between the
judges of the Court of International Justice, as appears in
paragraphs 49–54 of the opinion of the Court.

In denying redress to the plaintiff in *Kentucky v. Dennison*
(1861), the Court did not mention the earlier boundary cases
or their rationale, but addressed itself to the language of the
federal statute, which implemented the Constitution's command that a person, charged as was Lago, who is "found in
another State, shall on demand of the executive authority of
the state from which he fled, be delivered up" to that state.
The statute made it "the duty of the executive authority of
the State" on which such demand is made to cause the
fugitive to be delivered to the agent of the demanding State.
But the Court held that "the words 'it shall be the duty' were
not used as mandatory and compulsory but as declaratory of
a moral duty which this compact [the Constitution] created."
It noted that neither the statute nor the Constitution provided
means for compelling execution of the duty or punishment
for nonexecution. (One might think these within the armory
of any court.) And it even said that it was "clear that the
Federal Government, under the Constitution, has no power to
impose on a State officer, as such, any duty whatever." While
here the statutory duty "evidently points to the duty imposed
by the Constitution," the performance of it "is left to depend
on the fidelity of the State Executive to the compact entered
into with the other States. . . . If the Governor of Ohio

refuses to discharge this duty, there is no power delegated to the General Government, either through the Judicial Department or any other department, to use any coercive means to compel him."

The opinion talks in terms of the defendant governor, but the duty is certainly, by the Constitution, a duty of the state. It may be doubted whether the statute could enfeeble it into a duty solely of "fidelity" of the "chief executive authority of the state." Tho the Constitution is said to create only a moral duty, one wonders whether a proceeding against the state itself might not have been, indeed might not even today be, successful. But such a proceeding is unlikely, since extradition today is almost always based on the mandatory Uniform Criminal Extradition Act, now law in nearly every state.

The governor of the defendant state received the same deference when Louisiana sued Texas and officers of Texas (1900); as against the governor the Court dismissed the demand of Louisiana on the ground that the enforcement of quarantine against shipments from New Orleans was "political"; but the Court also found that the complainant lacked standing. And it held that the state itself was not liable because it had done nothing; its health officer had exceeded his authority.

Possibly the distinction made in this foggy case between the governor and the other defendants expresses an immunity or partial immunity accorded by courts to the chief executives of both nation and state and to legislatures, organs of government coordinate with the courts, in recognition of their importance—a sort of diplomatic status. Certainly the issue itself could not be political with respect to the governor yet fail to be political with respect to the Texas commissioner of health or the State of Texas itself. But to accord immunity to an officer when the state itself is not immune is incongruous. Nevertheless the propriety of suing the governor seems questionable unless he has done or ordered to be done the act complained of or has been charged by statute or constitution to do the act the nonperformance of which is the ground of suit. Every obligation of the state is not ipso facto that of the governor (or any particular officer).

There is no doubt that *state* law may require particular state officers, including the governor, to perform the state's duties, particularly duties with respect to other states. Any state thus can, as it does by enacting the Uniform Criminal Extradition Act, make what the Court in *Kentucky v. Dennison* called the governor's duty of fidelity into a legal duty. So long as there is no conflict with constitutions (or valid federal statutes) the legislature by statute or by compact with another state may impose duties on its own state or any officer of that state. And federal law within constitutional bounds may impose them on the state with or without designating who is to do them. In the area of interstate cooperation in enforcement of law, including rendition of accused persons, obligations more embracing than those of the United States Constitution have been enacted by states by compact or by uniform statutes, and have been applied by the courts. [*Gulley v. Apple* (Ark. Sup. Ct. 1948), *In re Cooper* (Cal. Sup. Ct. 1960), which the Supreme Court, tho requested, refused to review]. In enforcing duties of this sort a state may be plaintiff [*New York v. O'Neill* (1959)], and, at least if they spring from a compact, it is probable that a state as well as a private person or a state officer (as in the above cases), may be defendant.

Tho the political issue cuts a bold figure in the area of foran relations [*Banco Nacional v. Sabbatino* (1964)], it is an increasingly modest and hazy limitation on judicial handling of relations between states of the Union or between a state and the Union.

The Swiss Tribunal early recognized and still recognizes that some questions are political rather than legal [*Neuchâtel v. Confederation* (1879), *Confederation v. Urban Basel* (1939)]. Made political by the Swiss Constitution itself, Article 113, paragraph 3, is the whole field of discord between the Constitution and *federal* legislation (including treaties). But regarding executive action, both federal and cantonal, the Federal Tribunal exercises control. Also it deals with the question whether *cantonal* legislation conflicts with the national Constitution. That compacts (concordats) may be judicially disregarded if they conflict with the Constitution is probable.

A merely semantic disposal of the problem of defining what is political is made by Margrit Gut, who has said in her detailed study of intercantonal litigation, *Staatsrechtliche Streitigkeiten zwischen den Kantonen und ihre Beilegung* (1942): "Mere political questions between cantons are not properly called controversies; all intercantonal controversies [in the sense of the Constitution and statutes] are legal controversies" (p. 19). Article 113 of the Constitution and Article 83 of the Judicature Act—already quoted—seem to say almost the reverse; that is, that every case presented by a canton is ipso facto a controversy, but the plaintiff canton fails on the merits if by federal law the defendant's conduct was within its political discretion.

In contrast to *Kentucky v. Dennison,* Swiss law places all the relations of judicial assistance, including extradition of accused persons, within the area of enforceability by suit between cantons. The duty of collaboration between cantons was first declared by Articles 49 (civil cases) and 55 (criminal cases) of the 1848 Constitution, now, revised, Articles 61 and 67 of the 1874 Constitution. A federal statute concerning civil cases followed in 1852; and, with the development of federal penal law, a similar statute requiring cantonal authorities to assist in the enforcement of federal penal law was enacted in 1893. In the present Swiss system, nearly all penal law is federally enacted, but most of it is enforced through cantonal prosecution in cantonal courts. The Swiss Penal Code, Article 352, provides for cooperation in the broadest terms: "In every case under the present code or any other federal law, the Confederation and the cantons, and the cantons among themselves, are bound to assist one another." This long-standing duty of intercantonal assistance has been enforced in many cases between cantons, turning on a variety of issues.

The most unusual of these in the present century related to a request by Luzern for assistance from Nidwalden in prosecuting a man for fishing without authority from Luzern in a part of the Lake of the Four Forest Cantons, over the control of which Nidwalden and Luzern were in dispute. In this legal assistance case the court did not adjudicate the boundary, since neither canton then desired to submit that question. It declared that since Luzern did not prove that it had either de jure or de facto sovranty in the area, Nidwalden was justified in refusing Luzern's demand for investigation of the accused's conduct in waters to which Luzern alleged its law to extend [*Luzern v. Nidwalden* (1927)].

The obligation of intercantonal judicial assistance is not limited to criminal law administration. It covers all legal proceedings. It goes far beyond the simple requirement of Article 61 of the Constitution that "Final judgments in civil cases rendered by a canton are enforceable thruout Switzerland." Similarly statutes and judicial decisions have expanded the simple requirement of Article 67 that "Federal legislation shall provide for extradition of accused persons from one canton to another."

For enforcement of these duties by a canton's suit, the canton must have an interest of its own: ordinarily it must be a party to the pending or prospective litigation. This element is present in all penal cases, but, with respect to other cases, the standing of one canton to demand assistance from another depends on circumstances.

In the United States, the constitutional requirement (Art. 4, sec. 1) that "Full Faith and Credit shall be given in each State to the public Acts, Records, and judicial Proceedings of every other State" has not lacked judicial support as has the provision that fugitives from criminal trial and punishment should "be delivered up" by one state on demand of another. But there are no such cases in which both parties are states.

The Swiss Tribunal, however, has acted frequently at the behest of a canton to require another canton to respect the first canton's interest in nonpenal matters. Thus, when a woman domiciled in Zurich had been declared incompetent and confined there, as authorized by federal statute, because of prostitution, but had escaped to Geneva, Zurich was successful in suing Geneva (1925), which had not confined her, to obtain her return. The Tribunal considered the absence of any federal statute covering rendition of such persons immaterial, and said:

In civil cases, despite the language of Article 61 of the Constitution [which refers only to judgments] assistance has been extended to all steps preceding judgments. . . . In levies of execution, tho statute law is silent, officers of the several cantons are bound to help one another. In the levy of execution Switzerland is a single jurisdiction. . . . Intercantonal assistance in matters of wardship is based on the same reasons . . . tho not expressly provided for [by statute].

Similarly, three years later the Luzern (City) Probate Authority was successful in making the Executive Council of Vaud deliver a will in the custody of a Vaud attorney to the Authority, which was administering the estate of the testator; and Rural Basel was successful in making a Bern court enforce a fine imposed on a Bern attorney by a Basel court.

These last two cases were not original cases between cantons; according to the Swiss classification, they were review proceedings, actions to set aside erroneous executive decisions. The distinction is unimportant; they testify to the obligation of cooperation. Moreover, tho at one time the Tribunal insisted on the distinction, later it allowed a canton which had mounted a review action to ride on to victory by changing in midcourse to an original action [*Valais v. Zurich* (1945)].

A striking example of one canton's requiring another to honor the orders of the first is afforded by *Obwalden v. Zurich* (1949), a contest over the custody of an illegitimate son of a woman domiciled in Obwalden. The mother wished the child to be brought up by a family in Zurich, with whom she left the child and with whom he lived during the long court contest. The Federal Civil Code requires the proper cantonal wardship authority to appoint a temporary guardian for every illegitimate child; his permanent custody is later determined in legal proceedings. The Obwalden wheels of government moved accordingly. The responsible local wardship authority decided that the child should be placed in a Roman Catholic home, since the mother was of that faith.

Zurich requested a transfer of wardship to it, but Obwalden refused (as it lawfully could, with or without reason) and it demanded that Zurich turn the little boy over to the permanent guardian who had been apointed by the Obwalden court, contrary to his mother's wishes. But Zurich refused to honor Obwalden's repeated formal demand for the child.

The boy had lived three years with the Zurich foster family when Obwalden sued Zurich in the Federal Tribunal to compel surrender. That court, after unsuccessfully attempting mediation, ordered him transferred according to the lawful demand of Obwalden. The court explained that its order might be attributed to Article 61 of the Constitution or to "the common law principle that all cantons have to help one another carry out federal law." The regularity of Obwalden's conduct was beyond question, and the Tribunal, pretty clearly with reluctance, applied the rule of intercantonal cooperation despite its harshness on the persons concerned.

In the United States, such a question would be settled by suit between individuals. No common law principle would enable states or their organs to sue, and no statute or compact governs interstate relations in such matters. The law applying would not be interstate (federal common) law, but the law of some one state.

The most litigated of duties of cooperation between Swiss cantons is the duty to provide succor for indigents. The Federal Tribunal has established the rule that a canton must provide medical and other basic needs of any person within its territory who is unable to afford them. These outlays, however, are frequently reimbursable in whole or in part by another canton with which the recipient of the aid has a connection. This rule has been developed out of Article 45 of the Constitution, guaranteeing to Swiss citizens freedom to reside in any part of the country, but allowing this residence of a confederal to be terminated by the canton of residence if he is "repeatedly convicted of serious offenses" or becomes "a permanent charge" on the public.

Expulsion of confederals from a canton is allowed subject to the constitutional rule that their home canton must first be invited to provide support (i.e., reimburse the canton supplying it), and only if it refuses, may they be returned thither.

Conversely to the Constitution of the United States, whose Fourteenth Amendment makes citizens of the United States "citizens of the state wherein they reside," so that state citizenship is relatively unimportant, the Swiss Constitution makes every citizen of a canton a Swiss citizen. The term "home canton" or "canton of origin" is used to mean the canton of citizenship, a relationship not impaired by residence in another canton or abroad, but one that may exist with respect to more than one canton.

The cases between cantons concerning these matters show the development of rules of law by intercantonal litigation. Examples, to be discussed hereafter, are (1) the much criticized rule that if a family in which there are children of the mother's first marriage (who have the cantonal citizenship of their father) whose citizenship differs from that of their mother's second husband, becomes a permanent charge in another canton, these stepchildren of the second husband may be sent away to their canton of citizenship if that canton declines to pay for their support to the canton of their stepfather's abode; (2) the rule that, tho persons in only temporary need must be cared for by the canton where the need arises, without reimbursement by their home canton, yet a frontier canton, which destitute citizens of another canton enter from abroad, is entitled to be reimbursed by their canton of citizenship for their temporary support and hospitalization (including burial if they die); (3) the rule that if reimbursement of expenses of caring for a person who has multiple cantonal citizenship is due, the several cantons of which he is a citizen shall carry this burden equally. The last of these examples expressly overruled many earlier decisions.

In the United States, controversies of this sort are settled—or left to rankle—without benefit of judicial aid. No case between its states resembles these numerous Swiss cases.

The closest analogy, it seems to me, in the Supreme

Court—and it is not close—is the long litigation between Virginia and West Virginia over Virginia's demand that West Virginia assume an equitable share of the state debt of undivided Virginia, as it was when the northwestern counties split off to become the new State of West Virginia. Virginia here successfully asserted a contractual claim for such exoneration (and perhaps would have prevailed even without the rather fictitious contract that the Court enforced) somewhat as a canton may successfully assert a contractual or a quasicontractual claim to be reimbursed by another canton for assistance it has supplied to the latter's citizen in permanent need.

COMPACTS AND CONTRACTS

Several of the poor-relief cases involve intercantonal concordats or international treaties. One of these concordats or compacts changes the ultimate liability for public assistance afforded to citizens of one canton who, after establishing residence in another, become permanent charges there. The hardship of deportation to the home canton is abolished for those already established for four years, and the cost of assistance is split between the home canton and the canton of residence. The compact also provides that controversies concerning its application shall be settled not by the Tribunal but by the Federal Department of Justice and Police. Probably because a considerable number of cantons are parties to this compact, intercantonal court cases concerning indigents are less frequent now than they were a decade ago.

Claims involving intercantonal or international treaties are not confined to poor-relief litigation. Boundary cases involve them again and again in both countries. So, usually, do servitude cases, and cases regarding watercourses.

Such a compact was a mjaor factor in *Pennsylvania v. New Jersey* and in *Delaware River Joint Toll Bridge Commission v. Colburn,* both decided by the Supreme Court on the same day in 1940. The compact between Pennsylvania and

New Jersey, said the Court in the latter case, set up a commission, which it authorized

> to build bridges across the Delaware River between the two states, and for that purpose gave the Commission authority to acquire real property by purchase or by the exercise of eminent domain. . . . The present suit is a proceeding of mandamus, brought in the New Jersey Supreme Court to compel the Commission to . . . award compensation to respondents for damages to their land [caused by] the construction of the abutment.

The New Jersey court awarded compensation, but the Supreme Court reexamined the compact and the related statutes of Pennsylvania and New Jersey and concluded that no compensation was due to owners of land not acquired.

Having so decided the landowner's suit, the Court dismissed Pennsylvania's complaint in the original jurisdiction suit between the states "as the questions sought to be presented in this suit . . . have been determined" by the Court's disposition of Colburn's suit. Here was a situation where the issue was appropriately litigated by either type of suit. The Court favored the appellate action by dignifying its settlement with the long opinion.

An earlier suit based on a compact was *Kentucky v. Indiana* (1930). Here, too, there was a related case, pending in a Kentucky court, between individuals, but the Court concluded it would proceed to dispose of the interstate case since it raised issues that would not be reached in the other case. But if the private parties' case, tho in a state court, may produce a determination that will conclude the interstate case, the Court prefers to postpone the latter [*Arkansas v. Texas* (1953)].

The Supreme Court has pointed out (as have Swiss writers) that an agreement between states is not inevitably a compact. It may be a mere contract; that is, not deal with political interests. A true compact is valid only with the approval of Congress [U.S. Const. Art. 1, sec. 10, par. 3]. In Switzerland too it must be submitted to a federal organ, the Council [Swiss Const. Art. 7]. But the latter's approval is not essential [*Zurich v. Glarus* (1928)]. The distinction between a contract and a compact (which has political significance and often legislative effects) has not been clearly drawn in either country. It is discussed at some length, however, in *Virginia v. Tennessee* (1893), where the Court said that an interstate agreement for a mere *survey* of a boundary line would not require congressional consent.

Obviously, countless minor agreements between states or between cantons are made every year without consideration by the Congress or the Federal Council, respectively.

A state may not recover by relying merely on rights of its citizen. In *New Hampshire v. Louisiana* (1883), the Court unanimously refused to entertain a suit by a state to obtain payment of a bond of the defendant state when a citizen of the plaintiff was the "real party in interest," since this would be an evasion of the Eleventh Amendment. But when South Dakota, a donee with indisputable title to negotiable bonds issued by North Carolina, sued the latter state, the Court gave the plaintiff judgment (1904). Four justices dissented. There was no question of congressional consent to the creation of the obligation since it was not an interstate agreement; neither was its assignment to the plaintiff. The dissent is based in part on the imagined ground that the Court's decision would allow a state to collect the claim of anyone against the United States (as if that would cause the heavens to fall!) "if only a State chooses to acquire [it] and prosecute its enforcement." I call this ground imagined because, as was shortly afterward unanimously decided [*Kansas v. United States* (1907)], the suability of a state by the United States is not reciprocal.

The constitutional right of one state to sue another on a contract claim, tho acquired by assignment or negotiation and not by direct contracting between the states, has not since been questioned. Nor has it been confirmed. No similar Swiss cases are reported.

Presumably too a state or a canton can sue another—or any other person—on a contract or compact of which it is not a maker but is a "third party beneficiary."

SUITS ON COMMON LAW DUTIES

Ordinary tort claims may arise between states. Interfering or allowing interference with the natural flow of streams has been the basis of claims by lower against upper riparian states. Polluting or allowing pollution of moving air or water has provoked suits by other states affected. Helvetian controversies over water (the generation of hydraulic or hydroelectric power) have now been legislated out of the Tribunal into the Council [*Fribourg v. Federal Council* (1952)]. But earlier cases between cantons came before the Tribunal. In the United States, water litigation between states has chiefly concerned appropriation of water for irrigation or human consumption. The Court has frequently shied at this sort of controversy, saying that it could better have a legislative than a judicial solution, but, with or without the aid of statutes or compacts, it has adjudicated nevertheless.

The proper solution of the problem of fair division of water or restriction of pollution between states in the absence of federal statutes is almost as fluid as the water. Many of the cases have lasted decades; and so long as rains fall and the number of men increases, the problem will yield no final solution. Here the Supreme Court has to be the apportioner of a fugitive and fluctuating resource until some other form of administration is devised by Congress.

In an early one of these cases, *Kansas v. Colorado* (1902 and 1907), the Supreme Court twice spoke of itself as "sitting as it were as an international as well as a domestic tribunal," a description that offended Professor F. J. Berber (*Rivers in International Law* [1959], pp. 174–76) whose views will be examined more fully in the next chapter. Even if the Court were sitting as an international court, Berber thinks such decisions improper, as decisions that are political rather than legal, or, to use the language of the statute of the International Court of Justice, as decisions ex aequo et bono; that is, equitable, political, moral, rather than legal, in their nature.

Clearly the decisions in these water apportionment and water pollution cases are on the borderline between law and politics, with the Court operating in an area not only legally little charted, but not chartable in any detail because of the wide variety of values that a court should consider in each case in reaching its judgment.

According to Berber, if the Supreme Court were "sitting . . . as an international tribunal," it should have decided that every riparian state could take (or pollute?—he does not discuss this) a river as it pleases; the lower state has no *right* to anything; it has just what the upper state allows to flow down.

But a standard of fair or equitable apportionment and sometimes other standards have been espoused by many learned expounders of international law and embodied in treaties (not to mention the interstate decisions in Switzerland and the United States, which are wholly rejected by Berber as precedents for international action). Having recently examined the sources, William W. Van Alstyne, a thoro student of this question who differs from Berber, "on balance" concludes that "the unifying principle of equitable apportionment . . . enjoys sufficient authoritative support, and is sufficiently coherent, in its application to disputes involving economic interests in international rivers, to render such controversies justiciable according to international law."

I have quoted the last sentence of Professor Van Alstyne's well-pondered and carefully researched article on "The Justiciability of International River Disputes," published in the *Duke Law Journal* in 1964, in which, comparing the legality of the two important but vague concepts—equitable apportionment of rivers, and due process of law—he opines that, like due process, "equitable apportionment may reasonably be regarded as an emerging law, wholly susceptible of judicial application, even though it is not encapsuled in a verbal formula possessing the ingratiating clarity of a simpler, more rigid principle" (p. 338).

But he would not reject simpler principles that have been

put forth as rules of law, such as priority in time of water use, and others—and some not so simple, such as superiority of quality of some uses over others, or comparative dependence of the several claimant states on the use of the river's water. For they "are obviously relevant"; but "in the equitable apportionment of an international river treated as an integrated whole, as such a river should be," they are not "independently conclusive." In the next chapter we shall return to these water-flow cases, which in both countries—as well as in India [Const. Art. 262]—have been considered not entirely suitable for determination by regular courts. Thus Van Alstyne hesitates when he says:

It is clear, of course, that [an international] court cannot directly dictate the particular terms of an agreement between [states]. It can only pass on the validity of one party's objection to the position that the other party has taken. But in testing the position of each party against the principle of equitable apportionment, the court clearly influences negotiations by its anticipated decision on the validity of the complaining state's objections. (p. 339)

I do not think this rather roundabout statement that there is leeway in equitable apportionment comes to the right conclusion. To be sure, more than one way of allotting the river flow may be equitable—as more than one process of law may be due process of law. To be sure, courts should not decide such disputes (or perhaps any disputes) in greater detail than there is need to decide them. But if either party, to avoid more trouble, desires a very precise settlement, surely a court should meet this demand by setting standards of conduct in detail. As courts often do in boundary cases, nuisance cases, picketing cases, they should no less in water apportionment cases fix details to the degree necessary to end the controversy. This was what the Supreme Court was preparing to do if West Virginia did not pay the obligation which the Court said that that state owed to Virginia. It is what the court has done many times in the *Lake Level* case and other water cases, sometimes to overcome foot-dragging compliance, sometimes because conditions of weather, climate, or consumption necessitate new measures of detail to make operative the standards that the Court has previously announced. Whatever the correct rule of international law may be, the rule between cantons and between states is the rule of "fair" apportionment of use, applied in whatever degree of detail may be necessary to achieve settlement.

The relative rarity of suits between states (other than territorial and water disputes) in which the *plaintiff* is successful in comparison with those between Swiss cantons that are won by the complaining party is attributable in part, it seems, to the circumstance that the canton has liability for conduct of individuals that is greater than that of the American state—more like that of an international state in international law—for what happens within its boundaries. For an illustration of this let us return to the litigation between Solothurn and Aargau.

In 1900 the Tribunal gave relief to Solothurn when it sued Aargau because, as it alleged, persons within its boundaries suffered danger from a rifle range maintained not by the defendant canton but by Aarau, a city of that canton. The aggrieved state's right to relief for such conduct is established also by American cases, such as *Georgia v. Tennessee Copper Co.* (1907) (fouling of air by sulphurous smoke); *Pennsylvania v. West Virginia* (1923) (restriction by state statute of export from defendant's territory of natural gas); *New Jersey v. New York City* (1931) (fouling of ocean by dumping of garbage); and *Georgia v. Pennsylvania R.R.* (1945) (excessive rates for carriage of goods to and from stations in Georgia). But in all of these Supreme Court cases the alleged wrongdoer was the defendant. In *Solothurn v. Aargau,* it is not explained why the canton rather than the city of Aarau was the defendant. Aarau is not treated as the agent of Aargau; the theory seems rather to be that Aargau is answerable to a neighbor canton for allowing the dangerous shooting range to exist in its territory, as one owner of land would be liable to adjoining owners for such a "nuisance." This greater responsibility for what happens in cantonal territory that distinguishes Swiss interstate law from Ameircan is again illustrated by the will case brought by the Luzern

Probate Authority and by the custody case between Obwalden and Zurich.

The rifle range case reminds one of the well-known *Trail Smelter* arbitration between the United States and Canada, which, tho an international case, professed to draw support from *Solothurn v. Aargau* and several interstate decisions of the Supreme Court in concluding that Canada was liable for damage to property in the United States due to sulphur fumes released by a privately owned smelter in Canada. While the Supreme Court has held states liable to other states for allowing diversion or pollution of water, no smog or fume case against a state has yet been litigated.

The *Trail Smelter* case yielded a recovery of damages as well as an order to stop polluting, while Solothurn and the successful American states got only specific redress, no damages apparently being asked. But in *North Dakota v. Minnesota* (1923), where they were asked on behalf of landowners who had been damaged, the Court held the Eleventh Amendment forbad recovery.

The fact that there is a larger number of Swiss than American cases may be explained also as part of the greater expression in Swiss law of the doctrine of conflict of competences (the idea that either state A or state B is competent—not both—and that the court determines which). In the United States multiple taxation, multiple administration of estates, multiple authority to punish a single crime, have been deemed political rather than legal problems. The states have scarcely troubled the Court with them and have settled them, if at all, by nonjudicial devices such as reciprocal statutes, or by common law comity of state courts—within certain federal legal bounds (res judicata, full faith and credit, prohibition of double jeopardy, jurisdictional due process of law).

The objection that a specific claim is political is often stated by the Supreme Court in terms of the plaintiff's lack of standing to sue. A lack of standing *may* mean that the state's interest in the performance of defendant's legal duty is too remote—as, for example, was held in the much criticized decision of the International Court of Justice in 1966 concerning Southwest Africa, or in the Supreme Court's disposition of *New Hampshire v. Louisiana* (1883)—but often it is really that the alleged wrong is not a violation of a duty that is presently felt to be legal, tho it might be made such by legislation or by compact.

Thus, in *New Jersey v. Sargent* (1926), the Court, in granting a motion to dismiss New Jersey's bill against the Attorney General of the United States to prevent enforcement of the Federal Water Power Act, declared that the complaint "does not show that any right of the state, which in itself is an appropriate subject of judicial cognizance, is being, or about to be, affected." The Court quotes with approval the concurring opinion of Justice Thompson in the early case of *Cherokee Nation v. Georgia* (1831): "It is only where the rights of persons or property are involved, and when such rights can be presented under some judicial form of proceedings, that courts of justice can interpose relief." This does not elucidate when the Court will recognize the plaintiff's standing, but, after contrasting to this case Pennsylvania's successful suit to prevent West Virginia's restriction of extrastate delivery of natural gas, the Court disposes of the bill on the ground that "what it shows falls on the other side of the jurisdictional line," chiefly, it seems, because New Jersey did not make out that there had yet been or was about to be some application of the act that would invade power reserved by the Constitution to the states.

Perhaps *New Jersey v. Sargent* stands only for the rule that, for any suitor to prevail, he must allege that injury has occurred or is clearly imminent. This is certainly the reason why another original suit was dismissed which concerned the same federal statute. With the United States as plaintiff and West Virginia one of several defendants, the Court denied relief (1935) on the plaintiff's showing that the state had licensed the construction of a dam, the licensing of which construction, as the United States claimed, was within the exclusive authority of the Federal Power Commission. Distinguishing *United States v. Utah* (1931), a suit to quiet title to the bed of a river, because there "the public assertion of the adverse claim of the defendant out of possession is itself an invasion of the property interest asserted by the plaintiff," the Supreme Court dismissed the case against West Virginia because the bill presented "no justiciable controversy." It declared that tho "control of navigation by the United States may be threatened by the imminent construction of the dam," it is not sufficient "in point of definition of threatened injury and imminence of the controversy" to allege only that "permission to construct it" has been granted by the state. In other words, suit against impending constructors of the dam would lie, but not suit to cancel a state license to construct it.

The reluctance of the Supreme Court to entertain suits between states—in contrast to the attitude of the Federal Tribunal—is expressly avowed in *Alabama v. Arizona* (1934), where Alabama attacked the laws of Arizona and other states that prohibited sale of goods made by prisoners, tho Congress had declared that such laws did not conflict with its power to "regulate commerce among the states." The Court said:

Its jurisdiction in respect of controversies between the states will not be exerted in the absence of absolute necessity. *Louisiana v. Texas* [in which the Court had said in 1900 that "there must be a direct issue between them, and the subject matter must be susceptible of judicial solution. And it is difficult to conceive of a direct issue between two states in respect of a matter where no effort at accommodation has been made"]. . . . Our decisions definitely establish that not every matter of sufficient moment to warrant resort to equity by one person against another would justify an interference by this court with the action of a State. . . . The threatened injury [must] be of serious magnitude and imminent. . . . The burden upon the plaintiff State fully and clearly to establish all essential elements of its case is greater than that generally required to be borne by one seeking an injunction in a suit between private parties. *Connecticut v. Massachusetts* [a water appropriation case, decided in 1931, which, using similar language, cites *North Dakota v. Minnesota* (1923), a flooding case, in which the Court said "the burden on the complainant state of sustaining the allegations of its complaint is much greater than that imposed on a complainant in an ordinary suit between private parties"].

Reluctance to adjudicate has various but often scarcely distinguishable aspects, which Professor Alexander M. Bickel commends as "the Passive Virtues" in his "Foreword" to one of the *Harvard Law Review*'s annual reviews of Supreme Court adjudication [*HLR*, 75 (1961), 40], constituting a "wide area of choice open to the Court in deciding when, whether, and how much to adjudicate." The Court's profession and practice of nonadjudication (most marked in controversies between states except boundary disputes) has little counterpart in the language and action of the Swiss Federal Tribunal—possibly in part because, unlike the Supreme Court, it actively essays to settle cases, even between cantons, by pretrial conciliation.

In many if not all instances, issues that states bring to the high courts might be settled in suits between individuals. The *Delaware River Bridge* cases (1940), involving interstate compact, illustrate this. So does *Hinderlider v. LaPlata Ditch Co.* (1938), also ruled by a compact (between Colorado and New Mexico concerning use of the waters of an interstate river). But is there reason to prefer a settlement by private suit rather than by interstate suit, such as the water-division cases (not based on any compact) of *Kansas v. Colorado* (1907) and *Colorado v. Kansas* (1944), where the pending private suits were ordered dismissed?

Likewise the issues in the cases of state-against-state concerning claims to territory could be settled in suits between rival owners "claiming lands under grants of different States," to quote the Constitution's phrase (Art. 3, sec. 2). But this head of federal court jurisdiction is "virtually extinct," "substantially obsolete," as a United States Court of Appeals said in *Schroeder v. Freeland* (1951); and the only two cases between claimants to the same land under grants from different states that have ever reached the Supreme Court, I believe, were decided a century and a half ago [*Pawlet v. Clark* (1815), *Colson v. Lewis* (1817)]. Presumably this is because the Supreme Court has never caviled at handling boundary litigation between states.

In cases concerning water diversion, the Court's reluctance takes one form that is purely verbal, a protest now and then that a national legislative or interstate compactual solution would be preferable to a judicial [*Hinderlider v. LaPlata Ditch Co.* (1938), *Colorado v. Kansas* (1943)]. (Charles Warren, the distinguished historian of the Supreme Court, when special master to take evidence in *Texas v. New Mexico*, achieved in 1939 a settlement by interstate agreement.)

But reluctance in another guise, that of a rule that in interstate cases an existing or imminent wrong of "serious magnitude" must be shown, appears even in water cases [*Missouri v. Illinois* (1906) (pollution), *North Dakota v. Minnesota* (1923) (flooding), *Connecticut v. Massachusetts* (1931) (appropriation for urban use), *New Jersey v. New York* (1931) (same), *Washington v. Oregon* (1936) (appropriation for irrigation), dissenting opinion in *Nebraska v. Wyoming* (1945) (same)]. Tho this is not a phrase of sharp meaning, it is a hurdle for the plaintiff in interstate adjudication—if it still exists, which is doubtful, since for the last thirty years no such language has been used by the Court.

In 1953 the Supreme Court for the first time recognized that a state may have a (federal) common law duty to another state not to induce breach, or prevent performance, by a third person of a contract between him and the latter state. Tho the merits of the case were never reached, the Court, when Arkansas applied for leave to sue Texas on such a claim, by five votes against four, "continued" the application to await the outcome of a suit already pending in a Texas court. The four dissenters wished to deny the application, but only because they objected to the device of tabling it till the Texas court reached a decision, which, it was obvious, might at the same time end the interstate litigation: "We think the Texas courts should be left to decide their state law questions without the threat implicit in keeping this case alive." The difference, then, between the majority and minority was merely one of procedure.

We have taken a bird's eye view of the geography of

litigation. Now it is time to come to earth and excavate the two biggest mounds—the territorial cases before the Supreme Court and the public assistance cases before the Federal Tribunal.

4 DISPUTES PRIOR TO 1875
AND LATER DISPUTES
CONCERNING BOUNDARY OR
RELATED TO TERRITORY

SWISS national history is commonly reckoned to date
from the Pact of Rutli between Schwyz (hence the name of
the country), Unterwalden, and Uri that was made in 1291,
almost half a millennium before the birth of the United
States. By the ensuing century the practice of mediation and
arbitration of political controversies between petty sovrans
and governmental bodies was becoming well established in
this part of Europe. Cities and rural communities of the
developing Swiss complex individually or collectively pressed
their neighbors to substitute such procedures for resort to
force. Their permanent diplomatic conference, the Diet—one
might call it the "General Assembly" of the vaguely united
cantons—as well as particular cantons specializing in mediation, furthered settlements of controversies between the more
truculent ones, and pressed them often into agreeing to accept the verdict of arbitrators chosen in various ways.

Such was the situation before the strains of the religious
wars that devastated neighboring countries almost sundered
the Swiss oath-fellowship. But the fellowship lived and grew,
despite the sectarian and political conflicts at home and
abroad, until the Napoleonic invasion in 1798.

Meanwhile disputes between British colonies in North
America were settled by the British Privy Council or by Chan-
cery. After independence the Thirteen States provided for
arbitral settlement mediated by the United States Congress

61

under Article 6 of the Articles of Confederation, until the Constitution gave birth to the Supreme Court with power to decide all—that is, all adjudicable (sometimes called justiciable)—controversies between states, at least all that were not transformed into subjects for national legislative action by the new plan of federalism.

Before the Supreme Court was confronted by its first case between states, the Swiss fellowship had toppled before Napoleon, who created his puppet state, the Helvetic Republic, in which cantons were downgraded from members of a confederation to administrative segments of a unitary state. In the first years of the new century Napoleon restored Swiss federalism and by this Act of Mediation (1802) empowered the Diet of cantonal representatives to adjudicate between cantons. In so doing they were to sit "as the Syndicate, in which each deputy has one vote and cannot be instructed" by the government of his canton. But the Syndicate did no significant business. With the restoration of Swiss independence, there was a return to the pre-1798 regime, but with a procedure of mediation and arbitration now expressly set forth in the Treaty of Alliance (of the cantons) of 1815. A score of cases were so arbitrated between 1815 and 1848, chiefly concerning questions of cantonality (cantonal citizenship, which is the basis of Swiss nationality), of territory, and of the effect of the fission of the canton of Basel into the "half" cantons of Urban Basel and Rural Basel, which occurred in 1833. (Three decades later the splitting of West Virginia from Virginia precipitated long litigation between them in the Supreme Court.) Controversies between cantons did not cease with the Constitution of 1848. Now the newly created Federal Tribunal was empowered by reference from the Federal Council to decide civil law disputes between cantons [Const. of 1848, Art. 101], and the two houses of the Federal Assembly to deal with "disputes between cantons in the public law area" [Const. of 1848, Art. 74, heading 16]. Settlement by arbitration continued as an alternate, and still does; but it has become rare since 1875, when the aggrandized Tribunal obtained power to adjudicate in the public law area also.

I have made no personal investigation of the records of intercantonal arbitrations or of judicial decisions before 1875. The Federal Tribunal decisions thereafter do not reveal that these earlier adjudications or arbitrations substantially contributed to the present law between cantons, however important they were as pathbreakers to the establishment of a permanent full-powered organ of adjudication.

This is equally true of the pre-Constitutional decisions between the British colonies or states that framed their new Constitution in 1787. By far the most important of them, a territorial dispute between Pennsylvania and Connecticut, was adjusted in 1782, pursuant to the Articles of Confederation, by commissioners who did not support their arbitral award with any opinion.

The opening pages of Charles Warren's essay, "The Supreme Court and Disputes between States" (published in *International Conciliation* and elsewhere in 1940 and 1941), set forth the political importance of the pre-Constitutional cases between states. These cases, however, framed no doctrines that apparently influenced the Supreme Court.

The earliest Supreme Court case that was entitled state against state, involved the boundary between New York and Connecticut (1799). Here New York unsuccessfully sued Connecticut in an attempt to halt a suit in Connecticut between individuals who claimed title to the same land under conflicting grants of the two states. Connecticut did not appear. Chief Justice Ellsworth apparently thought New York could not sue (or perhaps could not obtain this remedy) to support what he deemed a political right: "If the bill contains no averment of a right of soil in New York, I think it must be [held to be] defective; . . . in no case can a specific performance be decreed unless there is a substantial right of soil, not a mere political jurisdiction, to be protected and enforced." Justice Patterson, however, remarked: "But where will this feud and litigation end? It is difficult and painful to conjecture, unless this Court can, under the constitution, lay hold of the case to decide the question of boundary." However, he recorded no dissent from the Court's denial of the injunction to prohibit the continuation of the suit in the Connecticut court.

Next, New Jersey sued New York on a boundary claim in 1829. When New York failed to appear, Chief Justice Marshall took occasion (1831) to review earlier actions against states and announced that the Court had a right "to proceed to a final hearing," but he reserved the further "question of proceeding to a final decree." ("Justice Baldwin did not concur," it is noted; a few years later in *Rhode Island v. Massachusetts* [1838] he wrote a strong opinion supporting the Supreme Court's authority.) New York then demurred, which the Court considered to constitute appearance. Before argument on the demurrer was completed, the states settled their dispute by compact approved by Congress in 1834.

It was often debated at the start whether legislation was needed to enable the Court to deal with cases between states. This had been New York's position in the suit brought by New Jersey. But, as Charles Warren says in his excellent little book, *The Supreme Court and Sovereign States* (1924), Marshall's boldness, just "when Calhoun and South Carolina were maintaining their Nullification doctrines, and Georgia was refusing to obey the mandate of the court in the Cherokee Indian cases," in maintaining the Court's right to proceed in the absence of the defendant state "is an illustration of the potent influence which the court exerted in establishing the Constitution on a firm basis" (p. 40).

There were two Cherokee Indian cases in which Georgia defied the order of the Supreme Court. Both these cases were criminal prosecutions that Georgia had instituted in her own courts. Convicted there of violating Georgia law by acts done within Cherokee territory, the accused in each case appealed to the United States Supreme Court. The issue was whether Georgia's laws applied to persons in that reserved area. In the earlier of these cases, *Tassel v. Georgia* (not reported), Georgia, ignoring a stay order from the Court, carried out its death sentence of Tassel while the case awaited review by the Court. Tho Worcester, the accused in the later case, was heard and was successful in the Supreme Court (1832), Georgia carried out the Georgia court's sentence—of imprisonment—against him also, in disregard of the Supreme Court's mandate.

There has been defiance also in our day by state governors of orders of the United States courts (tho not directly of the Supreme Court) on the steps of Central High School at Little Rock, Arkansas, and on the campus of the University of Mississippi at Oxford. These governors and their legislatures repeated in substance what happened a century and a quarter earlier when Governor Lumpkin and the Georgia Legislature thwarted the Supreme Court. But the twentieth-century performances, unlike the earlier ones, were broken by force by the President.

The federal statutes of the earlier day provided no clear remedy for such rebellious conduct, and, to meet the crisis, none was devised by Congress. As for President Jackson, who was sympathetic with Georgia's desire to expel the Cherokees, he tendered no executive intervention to support the Court; and was quoted, thirty years later, on dubious recollection, to have remarked to those who called on him on behalf of Worcester, "John Marshall has made his decision; now let him enforce it." The actions by Georgia in the Cherokee cases were the most successful, tho not the only, examples of state defiance of the national courts.

In cases between states notable instances of disobedience have occurred in the twentieth century. In *Wyoming v. Colorado* (1940) the plaintiff petitioned to institute against the defendant a proceeding for contempt of court for violation of a Supreme Court decree concerning diversion of water of the Laramie River. Colorado having been directed by the Court to "show cause," its answer could not deny that more water than the decree allowed had been withdrawn, but alleged that Wyoming had suffered no harm by the excess diversion and had acquiesced in it. While the Court stated that the first allegation alone was no defense, it found, as to the second, that "there was a period of uncertainty and room for misunderstanding which may be considered in extenuation." Hence, the petition was denied.

A more famous instance of resistance to a decree was provided by West Virginia. Soon after Virginia seceded from the United States in 1861, her northwestern counties, loyal to the United States, seceded from Virginia and were admitted as a new state of West Virginia. In the litigation between the states concerning the division of the Virginia public debt as it existed when West Virginia seceded from the parent state, the Court declared in favor of Virginia [*Virginia v. West Virginia* (March 1911)], leaving the parties to reach agreement on details. As they failed to do so, the Court referred these matters to a master and, on the basis of his report, reached definite conclusions and issued its decree (1915). The West Virginia legislature repeatedly and deliberately failed to appropriate the money to satisfy this decree. Virginia then asked the Court to mandamus the West Virginia legislature to pay. While strongly insisting on West Virginia's duty to pay, the Court thought other means of enforcement should be considered and reserved "further action in order that full opportunity may be afforded to Congress to exercise the power which it undoubtedly possesses" (1918). It restored the case for further argument in the following year on three questions concerning how, under existing legislation, the decree should be executed. At this point, the West Virginia legislature complied with the decree.

Both these incidents of temporary disregard of Court orders in interstate cases occurred many decades after the events that center in the Cherokee Indian cases, to which we now return to pick up the story of adjudication between states concerning territorial claims.

While the defiant attitude of public opinion in several states had become manifest after the Court's decision of *Craig v. Missouri* in 1830 and had been hightened the same year by Senator Hayne's famous exchange of speeches with Daniel Webster, in which Hayne supported the doctrine of "nullification," the Court's decree in the *first reported* Cherokee case gave Georgia no opportunity for disobedience, for the decision was for Georgia.

This famous suit, started in the Supreme Court, is known as *Cherokee Nation v. Georgia* (1831). The substantive issue sought to be presented, the reach of Georgia law over the Cherokee Nation's territory, was the same as in the preceding *Tassel* case, which the Court did not hear, and in the subsequent *Worcester* case, which it did. The Cherokee Nation brought suit as a state against the State of Georgia, to establish its autonomy.

Since the Cherokee Nation was not a state of the Union, the Court discussed at length whether it was some other sort of state within the meaning of "state" as used in Article 3 of the Constitution, and concluded, Justices Thompson and Story dissenting, that it was not. (It was not till 1934 that the Court in *Monaco v. Mississippi* decided that the Constitution did not authorize it to entertain a suit by a foran state. The opinions in *Cherokee Nation v. Georgia* and other early dicta of the Court pointed the other way.)

Thereby the Court avoided the merits of the claim and a clash with the defendant, which was determined to expel the Indians. To do so was to violate a series of treaties made by the tribe with the United States (both before and after the adoption of the Constitution), which the Court held valid in the *Worcester* case the next year.

Another ground for the decision, besides the Cherokee Nation's lack of the statehood required by Article 3, was suggested by Chief Justice Marshall—that the plaintiff made a demand that was political rather than legal, that "to control the legislature of Georgia . . . savors too much of the exercise of political power to be within the province of the judicial department." This theme, mentioned but not relied on by Marshall, was a second ratio decidendi for Justice Johnson, but was ignored by Justice Baldwin, the third member of the majority.

A decade and a half after these decisions in the United States the central authority of the Swiss Confederation—tho not its judicial arm, which was not created till 1848—met

and overcame the defiance of several cantons in the Sonderbund war. This war, like that to overcome the secession of
the Confederate States of America a few years later, led to a
strengthening of central government. The Swiss Constitution
of 1848, creating a truly federal state, was precipitated by the
Sonderbund cantons' ineffective resistance of central authority, just as the Thirteenth, Fourteenth, and Fifteenth Amendments to the Constitution of the United States were among
the consequences of the unsuccessful venture of the Confederate States.

But refusal by a canton to obey an order that the Swiss
Federal Tribunal has addressed to it, is something yet, and
we may hope never, to be recorded. Indeed since its judgments in these cases are declaratory in form, one may say
that compliance has always been obtained without even is-
suing an order.

A boundary dispute between Rhode Island and Massachusetts brings us to the era of Chief Justice Taney; but the
spokesman of the Court in the crucial decision in this litigation was Baldwin. Taney, indeed, dissented, referring to Marshall's suggestion in *Cherokee Nation v. Georgia* that the
question was political. Contests over political jurisdiction
rather than ownership (Ellsworth's "right of soil") he con-
ceived (1838) not to be "within the grant of judicial power
contained in the Constitution." In so viewing a boundary
dispute, Taney stood alone. He participated and delivered
opinions at later stages of the litigation, but in its final
disposition in 1846, in favor of Massachusetts, Taney again
stated his objections. As the Court *dismissed* the case, albeit
on the merits, Taney concurred in the decree. But, he said, "I,
of course, express no opinion upon the merits of the controversy; and have not even deemed it necessary to be present at
the elaborate arguments."

Justice Story did not sit in this case, possibly because he
was a citizen of Massachusetts. But, as already mentioned,
abstention by a judge because he is a citizen of a litigant has
not been customary in the Supreme Court, tho it is mandatory in the Federal Tribunal.

Concerning this all-important case of *Rhode Island v. Massachusetts* (1838) I can do no better than to quote a passage from the masterly book, *The Function of Law in the International Community* (1933), by the late Sir Hersh Lauterpacht, who later served as judge of the International Court of Justice. "*Rhode Island v. Massachusetts*," he says (pp. 441–42):

constitutes an emphatic judicial affirmation of the jurisdiction of the Supreme Court in the face of the plea challenging its jurisdiction in regard to so-called political disputes. The case is one of the *loci classici* on the question of the distinctions between legal and political disputes, and the relevant portions of the argument and of the judgement may therefore be summarized in some detail. This was a Bill filed in 1832 by the State of Rhode Island against the State of Massachusetts for the settlement of the boundary between the two States. The Bill asserted the right of Rhode Island to the disputed territory over which, at the time of the filing of the Bill, the State of Massachusetts claimed and alleged to exercise sovereignty on the ground that it was included in charters from the Crown of England. The claim was mainly based on a subsequent delimitation of the frontier by commissioners acting under the authority of the two States. It was contended in the Bill that the proceedings of the commissioners were vitiated by numerous errors, and that the line designated by them had always been resisted by Rhode Island. The Bill asked for a restoration of the right of the latter to the disputed territory. Counsel for the State of Massachusetts moved to dismiss the Bill on the ground that the Court had no jurisdiction. He contended that, by virtue of the Constitution, the jurisdiction of the Court was limited to judicial matters to be decided by the application of law and equity; that it would be manifestly absurd to extend it to political disputes of the day; that, there being no law regulating the intercourse between the States of the Union, there was no rule for settling a controversy between two or more States; and that, until such law existed, the Court could entertain no jurisdiction, because the State being above or beyond the existing law was not amenable to any superior. "This Court," it was said, "has no jurisdiction, because of the nature of the suit. It is in its character, political; in the highest degree, political; brought by a sovereign, in that avowed character, for the restitution of sovereignty."

The Court refused to admit the relevance of these objections. As Mr. Justice Baldwin pointed out, in the last analysis the dispute resolved itself into a controversy as to the locality of a point three miles south of the southernmost point of the Charles river; i.e. "Whether the stake set up on Wrentham Plain, by Woodword and Saffrey (the Commissioners), in 1642, is the true point from which to run an east and west line, as the compact boundary between the States. In the first aspect of the case, it depends on a fact; in the second, on the law of equity, whether the agreement is void or valid; neither of which present a political controversy, but one of an ordinary judicial nature, of frequent occurrence in suits between individuals."

Lauterpacht then quotes from Justice Baldwin's opinion the well-known passage (12 Peters 657, 736) which, he says, gives "classical expression" to the test of what interstate disputes are judicable.

The founders of our government could not but know, what has ever been, and is, familiar to every statesman and jurist, that all controversies between nations, are, in this sense, political, and not judicial, as none but the sovereign can settle them. In the declaration of independence, the states assumed their equal station among the powers of the earth, and asserted, that they could of right do what other independent states could do; but they surrendered to congress, and its appointed court, the right and power of settling their mutual controversies; thus making them judicial questions, whether they arose on "boundary, jurisdiction, or any other cause whatever." There is neither the authority of law or reason for the position, that boundary between nations or states, is, in its nature, any more a political question, than any other subject on which they may contend. None can be settled without war or treaty, which is by political power; but under the old and new confederacy they could and can be settled by a court constituted by themselves, as their own substitutes, authorised to do that for states, which states alone could do before. We are thus pointed to the true boundary line between political and judicial power, and questions. A sovereign decides by his own will, which is the supreme law within his own boundary; 6 Peters, 714; 9 Peters, 748; a court or judge decides according to the law prescribed by the sovereign power, and that law is the rule for judgment. The submission by the sovereigns, or states, to a court of law or equity, of a controversy between them, without prescribing any rule of decision, gives power to decide according to the appropriate law of the case; 11 Ves., 294; which depends on the subject-matter, the source and nature of the claims of the parties, and the law which governs them. From the time of such submission, the question ceases to be a political one to be decided by the *sic volo, sic jubeo,* of political power; it comes to the court to be decided by its judgment, legal discretion, and solemn consideration of the rules of law appropriate to its nature as a judicial question, depending on the exercise of judicial power; as it is bound to act by known and settled principles of national or municipal jurisprudence, as the case requires. . . .

These considerations lead to the definition of political and judicial power and questions; the former is that which a sovereign or state exerts by his or its own authority, as reprisal and confiscation; 3 Ves., 429; the latter is that which is granted to a court or judicial tribunal. So of controversies between states; they are in their nature political, when the sovereign or state reserves to itself the right of deciding on it. . . .

The "political question" objection, as has been mentioned, was rejected again in the boundary controversies between Florida and Georgia in 1855 and between Virginia and West Virginia in 1870.

In the thirty-five years following Justice Baldwin's opinion, boundary cases—the two just mentioned plus *Missouri v. Iowa* (1849), *Alabama v. Georgia* (1860), and *Missouri v. Kentucky* (1871)—were the only interstate cases that were decided by the Court, with one exception. This exceptional case, to which reference has been made in the preceding chapter, arose on the eve of the Civil War. Kentucky sought to compel Dennison, the governor of Ohio, to render to Kentucky for trial a free Negro man, who was charged with "assisting a slave to escape" from her master in Kentucky. Certainly the Supreme Court could have easily ruled Governor Dennison's refusal a judicially redressable violation of Article 4 of the Constitution. But, presumably apprehensive of the political reaction to requiring the return to slave territory of such a person, the Court, as we have seen, interpeted this provision of the Constitution to be only hortatory.

Thus, up to 1875, the year in which the Swiss Federal Tribunal, in its modern form, came into being, no state had succeeded in obtaining from the Supreme Court redress in any case other than a boundary dispute. Both courts were soon called on for the decision of claims of wider variety. In this chapter, however, we focus on disputes concerning boundaries and other claims linked to territory, such as river flow. These continue for some time to be the most usual subject of litigation between states, but their frequency diminishes steadily. Also in Switzerland the quantity of boundary and other territory-related cases, always less than in the less settled country, has waned in the twentieth century. No boundary case has been decided there for over fifty years. And in the United States none till *Louisiana v. Mississippi* (1966), for over twenty years.

Water and river bank boundaries, as contrasted to boundaries by landmarks and metes, have concerned the Supreme Court many times since the first such case was decided on its merits (*Alabama v. Georgia*) in 1860. One of the most interesting of these was that which defined the state line in Delaware River and Bay between New Jersey and Delaware. Here Justice Cardozo wrote the opinion (1934), which set for the lower waters the main channel of navigation as the state line, in the absence of any "possessory act or other act of dominion to give to the boundary . . . a practical location or to establish a prescriptive right." But upriver, the Court held, within the New Castle (Delaware) twelve-mile circle, named in the deed of feoffment to William Penn from the Duke of York, which was confirmed by royal letters patent, the river was Delaware's as far as the normal low water mark on the Jersey side.

The Swiss Tribunal made similar determinations in two Rhine River boundary suits, already mentioned, between Zurich and Schaffhausen, awarding, on the basis of ancient grants, all the river to the latter in part of its course (1897), but fixing a center line boundary in another stretch (1907). These are the only two reported water boundary decisions by the Federal Tribunal.

Boundaries following streams sometimes have been set, depending on the language of grants, at other locations than the line of the thread (or of the main channel of navigation) or than the ordinary (low) water line on a bank. Thus in *Oklahoma v. Texas* (1921) the Court construed "bank" to mean not all land above the normal low water line, but only that beyond the base of the "cut bank," the line dividing the bare sandy floor, thru which the Red River meandered during most of the year, from the part of the valley that was higher and grass-covered; but in *Vermont v. New Hampshire* (1933) it rejected a similar claim of New Hampshire and set the boundary at the (low) water line on the Vermont shore.

The Court often has taken years to answer the various questions of fact and of documentary construction in boundary cases. As a means of settlement without resort to force, such cases institutionally are important; and they often concern great resources, such as oil under the river floor in the *Oklahoma-Texas* case and in *Louisiana v. Mississippi* (1966). Factually complex and hard fought, they provide little legal ambrosia. Brief mention of a few examples suffices.

The thread of the stream (thalweg) doctrine of international law was applied to interstate boundaries first in *Iowa v. Illinois* (1893) and has been frequently reiterated. Followed in *Minnesota v. Wisconsin* (1920), it was given the meaning of channel of navigation rather than line of greatest depth of water.

Soon after the Delaware River boundary case (1934), where the thalweg doctrine was reviewed historically and affirmed, the Court had to settle the boundary in Green Bay between Wisconsin and Michigan (1935), the last phase of a dispute over a boundary of several hundred miles. The act of Congress had designated as the boundary "the centre of the most usual ship channel of the said bay to the middle of Lake Michigan." But the Court found it impossible to identify any ship channel in so large and deep a bay. Since the controversy between the states was chiefly over fishing rights, the Court held for equal division of the water area.

Arkansas twice sued Tennessee over land avulsed by sudden changes in the course of the Mississippi. The claim of Arkansas, on the west bank, to "Centennial Island," now attached to the east bank of the river, was sustained in a series of decisions between 1918 and 1926. A few years later, Arkansas started another suit against Tennessee in which the principal decision was rendered in 1940. Here it claimed land that prior to 1821 was a peninsula on the west side of the river, but by a change in course in that year became an island and, with the silting up of the old channel, soon became attached to the Tennessee shore. While the avulsion of "Moss Island" did not alter the boundary, the Court found that the area had passed to Tennessee by the latter's exercise of dominion, at least since 1870, without contest by Arkansas, and that the gradual increase of Moss Island by accretion as the river shifted farther west also was Tennessee territory.

While the Supreme Court recognized the rule of acquisition by adverse political dominion as operative between states in the early case of *Rhode Island v. Massachusetts* (1838), the Swiss Federal Tribunal held that a "tacitly agreed modification of boundaries" could not be established by proof that construction in the disputed area of the Rhine had been authorized by the canton which was seeking to establish the modification [*Schaffhausen v. Zurich* (1897)]. The Tribunal noted the presence only of "administrative activity" and the absence of "any act of judicial sovranty" (implying perhaps that the latter might be effective). But it declared broadly: "The rule is that a modification of relations of sovranty once determined between cantons can be effected only by a formal treaty, one that is negotiated by the organs of the two cantons competent thereto, and moreover one that must be approved by the federal authorities."

Swiss Professor Max Huber, later a judge of the Permanent Court of International Justice, writing in the *American Journal of International Law*, 3 (1909), 62, said the Tribunal had thus held that the Swiss Constitution precluded acquisition of territory by prescription. But in 1907 (apparently after Huber had written and while his German manuscript was being translated into English) the Tribunal made a second decision, also concerning the Schaffhausen-Zurich Rhine boundary (but not the same part of it), in which it made a careful factual survey of Zurich's claim of acquisition by prescription, and, tho rejecting it on the facts, certainly differed from Huber's extreme interpretation of the Constitution. Parenthetically let me repeat, the Constitution has since been held to mean that intercantonal treaties are valid without the approval of the Federal Council [*Zurich v. Glarus* (1928)].

The two latest boundary cases decided by the Supreme Court should be mentioned. *Kansas v. Missouri* (1944) turns entirely on disputed facts concerning the shifting of the main channel of the Missouri River. This, indeed, is typical of boundary disputes; in both countries, they most often turn not on the meaning of language in private or public grants or statutes, but on its application, the dispute being about objective events or landmarks; so that usually, as the Court said in *Kansas v. Missouri,* "the states are not in dispute about the applicable law." *Louisiana v. Missippi* (1966) related to the interstate boundary in the Mississippi, at a point where its bed was peppered with oil wells. "At all times," said the Court, "the live thalweg has been the true boundary." But this for many years was steadily shifting eastward. So, measuring this shift, the Court set dates when particular wells formerly in Louisiana came within Mississippi.

But tho the doctrinal significance of boundary cases may be small, no type of case has evoked stronger emotions. "In at least four instances," says Charles Warren in "The Supreme Court and the World Court," *International Conciliation,* No. 289 (April 1933),

the questions involved in boundary disputes had given rise to the use of armed force by the citizens of the opposing States. Their settlement through judicial decision, therefore, has been of great import to the peace of this Nation. For instance, in 1849, the Court decided a boundary controversy between Missouri and Iowa which involved sovereignty over a valuable strip of territory of about 2,000 square miles—a tract about two thirds the size of Alsace. During this controversy (which had been pending for twelve years) Missouri at one time had called out 1,500 troops and Iowa 1,100, to defend their respective alleged rights. The conflict of claims was the more serious, by reason of the fact that if Missouri prevailed, these 2,000 square miles would become additional slave territory; if Iowa won, they would be free soil.

Controversies that had evoked violence were settled also by *United States v. Texas* (1896), *Louisiana v. Mississippi* (1906), and *Oklahoma v. Texas* (1921). Both in these boundary suits and in others "a state of facts was presented which, if arising between independent nations, might well have been a cause of war" (Warren, *The Supreme Court and Sovereign States,* p. 38).

Controversies concerning that fugitive but ever newborn natural resource, water, produce many cases, of which the first in the one country was *South Carolina v. Georgia,* decided in 1876, and the first in the other was *Aargau v. Zurich,* decided in 1878. In the former case the outcome was affected by federal action; federal officers were additional parties; and the claim of South Carolina was defeated by a federal statute.

Steadily in both countries control has been nationalized, in the European country by amendments of the Constitution relating to waterpower and accompanying legislation, in the American by increasing exertion by Congress of its authority over interstate commerce.

The Swiss development has been a transfer of much jurisdiction in intercantonal water controversies from the Tribunal to the Council, recognized by the Tribunal's decision in *Fribourg v. Federal Council* (1952). The American drift away from litigation about watercourses was favored by the Court's recognition that the United States is a necessary party in certain water-flow litigation, which makes suit impossible unless the United States consents. Contrast the Court's action in *Kansas v. Colorado* (1902 and 1907), where the Court dismissed the United States as a party (albeit after giving it full opportunity to be heard on the merits) in a case concerning water rights in the Arkansas River, with *Arizona v. California* (1931), where it held the United States to be an indispensable party in the determination of rights in the Colorado River, whose waters were to be confined by the Hoover Dam, constructed under authority of a federal statute.

Across the Atlantic, meanwhile, in 1926, Schwyz sued Zurich for allowing water of springs to be diverted in violation of intercantonal treaty. The Tribunal decided this claim without the Confederation's playing any part. Similar interstate river diversion cases have been settled by the Supreme Court in recent years; for example, the Boston water supply case, *Connecticut v. Massachusetts* (1931); or the North Platte River irrigation controversy, *Nebraska v. Wyoming* (1945), where the role of the United States was expounded by the Court. In the latter case neither Colorado, whence the river sprang, nor the United States had at first been held to be a necessary party (April 1935), but at later stages the

Court deemed that Colorado might be impleaded (Dec. 1935), and that the United States might intervene (1938).

The Supreme Court has, as we have noted, repeatedly said that a state was entitled to redress against another state only for wrongs "of serious magnitude." It has said so even in cases of this familiar type [*Washington v. Oregon* (1936)]. On this point the dissenting opinion in *Nebraska v. Wyoming* (1945) reviews all the earlier cases.

The state has an interest in many ways analogous to private ownership, but its right is distinct from, and, as the Court expressly said in *Hinderlider v. LaPlata Ditch Co.* (1938), superior to, the ownership rights of individuals. Individuals may sue one another, as they did in the last-named case, but the state also may sue, and it may sue another state rather than (or in addition to) private persons. If it does so, any suits of individuals are overridden by the suit brought by (and against) the states in which the water is utilized. Individuals' rights also, to some extent, may be altered or destroyed by interstate treaty. These views, set forth in the *Hinderlider* case, are repeated in the interstate case of *Colorado v. Kansas* (1943). But in *Schwyz v. Zurich* (1926) the Swiss Tribunal construes such a compact rather violently to avoid disturbing private rights in springs, tho not denying that a compact could displace such rights.

A series of cases, beginning with *Kansas v. Colorado* (1902 and 1907), lays down a rule of fair apportionment of waters between upper and nether states thru which a river flows. These cases deal chiefly with depletion of streams by withdrawing water for consumption in homes and factories (the cases relating to eastern rivers) or for irrigation (the cases relating to western rivers); while the Swiss cases center upon water for power (hydraulic or hydroelectric), a matter now largely under central legislative-executive control in both countries.

Before such central control so largely superseded state control, the courts of both countries took similar stands to allow reasonable utilization of water by the upper state or by persons in the upper state, and to prohibit its exhaustion by them. *Aargau v. Zurich* (1878) lays down this equitable apportionment rule. Another intercantonal case, *Aargau v. Solothurn* (1892), deals with taxation of waterpower. Later cases (not between cantons) turn on the effect of the federal waterpower act whereby control was transferred from the Federal Tribunal to the Federal Council. In the United States, federal authority, so long as unexerted, does not exclude interstate suits, as we have seen. While starting later, more interstate water litigation has occurred there than in Switzerland. Among the cases of the last half century are *Wyoming v. Colorado* (1922, 1932, 1936); *Connecticut v. Massachusetts* (1931); *New Jersey v. New York* (1931); *Colorado v. Kansas* (1943), an unsuccessful attempt to revise the decision in the pioneer case of *Kansas v. Colorado* (1902, 1907); and *Nebraska v. Wyoming* (1945). But congressional exercise of its power to regulate interstate commerce, in its aspect of interstate navigation (but actually geared principally to satisfy water needs in housekeeping, in industry, and in agriculture, to prevent floods, and to generate electric power) may preclude interstate suits unless the United States, as a necessary party, consents [*Arizona v. California* (1931)].

The line between law and policy or expediency is very foggy in water division cases. Absent treaties, it may be uncertain whether, between international states, one riparian state may take (or allow persons within it to take) water to the utter deprivation of the other. But it is clear that within both the Swiss Bund and the United States the rule of fair apportionment of water between states has emerged from such conflicts.

Also in federal Germany of the Weimar Republic. The German Staatsgerichtshof in the Danube case, *Württemberg and Prussia v. Baden* (1927), recognized that the "community of German states" was closer than the general community of nations so that (as translated by R. K. Baystone) "a greater restriction on the fundamental principles of sovereignty is reached in the relations of German states to each other than when two completely foreign states face each other. . . . From this arises the obligation of German states in relation to each other which are not at least in the same measure to be drawn from international law which is intended for all states." I quote from page 176 of *Rivers in International Law* (1959), by Professor F. J. Berber of the University of Munich, who supports sharp differentiation here between interstate intrafederational law and international law.

Nevertheless, the German court in 1927, like the United States Supreme Court in its series of cases apportioning water flow, but unlike the Swiss court half a century earlier, found some support for its decision in international law. The courts referred not to specific decisions but to the principle that there is a duty between states of reciprocal respect and consideration; that is to say, a duty not to injure one another. And reciprocally in 1933, the *Trail Smelter* arbitrators between Canada and the United States relied on these intrafederational precedents.

I incline to disagree with Berber's assertion that the principle of fair apportionment of river water "cannot be introduced into international law by the round-about way of the alleged application of international law in federal courts" (*Rivers*, p. 177). For rules developed as solutions of conflicts between intranational states may well be harbingers of the rules that govern the solution of disputes between fully sovran states. Certainly, as a "general principle" and source of international law [Art. 37 of the Statute of the International Court of Justice], a customary law between states of federacies, devised and applied by their courts, is at least as convincing as is a pattern of dealings between individuals, sanctioned by national courts.

Another sort of wrong connected with water that may be redressed by suits between states parallels the private law tort of nuisance. This is pollution. The Chicago River case, *Missouri v. Illinois* (1901 and 1906), was the pioneer. For lack of "serious magnitude" of the pollution the Court denied relief. But the still pending case concerning the Michigan-Huron lake level (*Wisconsin v. Illinois*, 1929 and later),

involving the reversal of flow of the Chicago River and including many states downstream (or downlake), evoked redress. New York's complaint against New Jersey (1921) for
polluting New York Harbor failed. But ten years later (1931)
the Court gave redress for sea pollution—when New Jersey
sued the City of New York. There the Court held that New
York City (by its own action, and not merely by its tolerance
of others' action) was infringing New Jersey's legal right to
have a somewhat pure ocean wash its shores. In none of
these cases was the United States held to be a necessary
party.

The interstate Ohio River compact came before the Court
in *West Virginia ex rel. Dyer v. Sims* (1951), in substance a
suit brought by an interstate agency against the state of West
Virginia. Here control of pollution and other interests had
been accorded by an interstate compact to the interstate
agency. In this suit to compel (an officer of) one of the party
states to perform its treaty obligations, the Supreme Court
reversed the state court and enforced the duty.

Pollution of water has not been the subject of intercantonal suits. But it clearly could be [*Sagitta Co. v. Solothurn*
(1958)]. Nor has pollution of air—a wrong held redressable
by suit in *Georgia v. Tennessee Copper Co.* (1907), where
the defendant was a business corporation, acting in another
state.

The Federal Tribunal entertained a somewhat similar action between two cantons (a city of the defendant canton
being the wrongdoer, as New York City was in the Atlantic
Ocean pollution case). This was the suit (1900), already
often mentioned, in which Solothurn obtained redress
against Aargau because the Argovian city of Aarau had set
up a rifle range so near the frontier that Solothurn claimed
its citizens were unjustly endangered by stray bullets. After
Aarau had rebuilt its range to provide greater safety, the
court modified (1915) the drastic injunction that it had
granted fifteen years before.

Twin interstate cases involving another natural resource
are *Pennsylvania v. West Virginia* and *Ohio v. West Virginia*

(1923), where the plaintiff states were successful in their prayer that West Virginia be ordered to cease requiring distributors (by pipe) of natural gas produced ("captured") in West Virginia to serve all buyers in that state before serving those in neighboring states. The plaintiff states succeeded thus in preventing the defendant state from limiting this (man-created) flow of gas from one state into others.

The main issue in these companion suits and in the controversy between Solothurn and Aargau could well be phrased as, what standing has a state to protect individuals' rights in commercial freedom, in the American cases, and in bodily safety, in the Swiss. But while in the cases against West Virginia the Supreme Court talks of freedom (from state hindrance) of the flow from state to state of goods in commerce analogous to freedom of the flow from state to state of rivers, as the legal basis for forbidding the trammels that West Virginia was imposing, the Federal Tribunal in *Solothurn v. Aargau* relies largely on the analogy of the law of easements between owners of adjoining land.

More recently the United States brought to the Court a controversy with several coastal states concerning rights in the land beneath their marginal ocean: *United States v. California* (1947), *United States v. Louisiana* (1950), *United States v. Texas* (1950). The Court had no hesitation in holding these disputes within its cognizance, but the justices were in sharp disagreement on the merits. The decisions, in favor of the United States, became a subject of hot political debate. A bill to "restore" the contested rights to the states was passed by Congress, vetoed by President Truman, passed again in 1953, and approved by President Eisenhower. Challenged in interstate litigation, the act was held constitutional [*Alabama v. Texas* (1954)].

If the contest between the United States and the states had been only over *ownership* of the ocean floor, as the minority saw it, the parties would have contested more nearly as equals, as they did in the Red River boundary dispute, *United States v. Texas* (1896), in *United States v. Utah* (1931), and in *United States v. Oregon* (1935), disputes over ownership of underwater land. But the contest was held by the majority of the Court to turn on the difference in quality of the interest of the parties. This qualitative difference of right, resting on the inequality of the suitors in most contests between a component state and the central state, distinguishes them so substantially from suits between component states that if mention of such cases is made, often, as now, it is only to exclude them from further examination.

5 INTERCANTONAL LITIGATION CONCERNING PUBLIC ASSISTANCE

THE predominant subject of Swiss intercantonal adjudication has been the obligation of public assistance to the needy. This has already been mentioned as exemplifying in many of its cases the jurisdiction of the Tribunal to settle competence conflicts. As the conflict is negative, each canton disclaiming its own liability, such cases often are assertions of quasicontractual rights (reimbursement of expenditures) by the canton that first gave succor to the indigent in need. Recovery is attributed to the civil law doctrine that one may obtain reimbursement for doing in appropriate circumstances for another business that benefits him. But the right between cantons is recognized as a public law right [*Urban Basel v. Solothurn* (1882)].

The basis of poor relief (except when modified by treaty) is cantonal citizenship (cantonality), not domicil or that enduring residence which in Anglo-American law is called settlement. But since the Constitution (Art. 45) with limited exceptions allows any Swiss to reside where he pleases—in a canton of which he is not a citizen he is known as a confederal—but allows him to be sent back to his home canton either for repeated crime or for permanent indigence requiring public assistance (for which his canton of citizenship has been invited but has refused to pay), the Federal Tribunal evolved the doctrine that the supplying or financing of public assistance to a confederal was a responsibility of his canton of citizenship only if his need was permanent. Temporarily any need must be cared for by the canton where this need first becomes manifest.

This rule was strengthened and generalized by considerations of humanity into a principle more basic than that of responsibility of the canton of citizenship—one that applies not only to confederals but also to aliens, that applies not only to residents but to nonresidents, that applies regardless of why the person is where he is when his need transpires. This principle is that it is the responsibility of the canton of his presence to take care of anyone known to be in need who is too poor to care for himself. The duty is described variously, as "linked to the mere fact of illness" (*St. Gallen v. Thurgau*, 1913), as (in the instance of an alien) "not so much a duty of international law or federal law as one that is characteristic of the modern state itself" (*Zurich v. Thurgau*, 1914), as "a duty of humanity . . . inhering in the function of the state . . . justified by the requirements of public order" (*Zurich v. Geneva*, 1925).

These statements of the Swiss court of the common law of humanity forecast the Universal Declaration of Human Rights, voted by the United Nations General Assembly in 1948, which, tho not a treaty, has been accepted as law in a number of countries. Its Article 25 declares:

Everyone has the right to a standard of living adequate for the health and well-being of himself and of his family, including food, clothing, housing and medical care and necessary social services, and the right to security in the event of unemployment, sickness, disability, widowhood, old age or other lack of livelihood in circumstances beyond his control.

But from American common law these principles are up to now absent. Nor has the Constitution of the United States been held to impose such a duty on the nation or the states. The "bill of rights" of their constitutions is a bill of prohibitions of positive wrongs, a bill of restraints on abuses of government that imposes no affirmative duties on government, such as the duty to succor persons in distress. All that American law offers are some statutory duties of succor running only to residents or settlers, not to all men, and assuring to the indigent migrant away from his state of settlement (if any) only the liberty to perish of starvation or disease. Of course there are private and public agencies that benevolently hinder the happening of extreme affliction; but such handling of the protection of human health and security is free enterprise in an unworthy dress. It is comparable to fighting fires by the hue and cry of a casual crowd.

If the plaintiff canton (or its town) provides relief to an indigent confederal that should be provided by the defendant canton (or town thereof) because his need is lasting, the supplying canton (having given the required statutory notice to the other canton) is entitled to reimbursement of its expenditures. The Federal Tribunal is often called on to determine such questions as (1) where the indigent was when first his need became manifest, (2) whether the need is "permanent," (3) whether the recipient confederal is a citizen of the canton sued, (4) what expenses are reimbursable. And issues arise also under intercantonal or international treaties.

The Federal Tribunal has sometimes overruled itself. Thus for a long time it held that, absent a treaty, a canton of citizenship could not recover from another canton of which also the recipient of aid was a citizen. This is the rule of international law for indigents of double nationality. But many cantons by treaties had introduced sharing of costs of maintaining persons of "double" cantonality who are in permanent need. Overruling earlier cases, the Tribunal acknowledged this rule as intercantonal common law [*Luzern v. Neuchâtel* (1947)].

The question immediately arose, whether in a case of multiple cantonality (as in cases of single cantonality) the canton providing assistance could obtain any reimbursement from the other canton of which the indigent, in this case an invalid woman, was a citizen, if that canton wished to have her returned to it. Perhaps because the standard of assistance was higher where the indigent was, she preferred to remain there; and the court ruled that it was her right to do so, since the Constitution prohibited cantons from expelling their own cantonals, and that the canton of her citizenship in which she chose to reside could recover half its outlay from the other canton [*Urban Basel v. Fribourg* (1951)]. Thus the canton which provides for the indigent's permanent need is entitled to half (or proportionate) reimbursement from the other canton (or cantons) of which the assisted person is a citizen.

Another modification of the division of liability for public assistance was a relaxation, in one situation of hardship, of the rule that costs of providing *temporary* aid must be borne by the canton where the need first becomes evident.

Under this rule if a cantonal of A while in canton B, because of recognizable illness or other mishap, falls into temporary distress and becomes unable to provide for the economic needs of himself and his family, canton B has to provide assistance without reimbursement. If he now goes for any reason into canton C, canton C has to provide assistance, but canton C, tho it cannot expel him, can get reimbursement from canton B where his need accrued. In short, the canton in which the person's temporary need develops, e.g., where onset of labor overtakes a pregnant woman [*Geneva v. Urban Basel* (1927) (elaborate dictum)], is liable for the whole of that need wherever the person may go.

But this is not the only rule regarding liability. Thus, if canton C unlawfully expels the indigent into canton D, then the cost to canton D of relieving his need will be recoverable by D from C. In other words, a rule of liability based on fault is recognized [*Zurich v. Schaffhausen* (1917)]. D could recover from C for its assistance to the indigent on the ground of C's fault, or from B as the canton where the need arose, if the indigent's need is temporary, but not from canton A. We may further speculate that if B pays D, B could not get reimbursement from C because C's fault was subsequent to the accrual of B's liability and no cause of it; and if C pays D, C could not recover over from B since C's misconduct bars C. These questions, however, have apparently not yet come to the Tribunal.

What has come to it and has caused it to recognize an exception to the general rule of liability for temporary need is the situation of the frontier canton faced with the giving of aid to indigent citizens of other cantons who enter from abroad. If the need had developed when they were within Switzerland, the canton where it developed could be billed for the costs. But the foran country is not liable for the care of an alien after he is properly returned to his homeland. Should the frontier canton or the canton of citizenship bear the expense?

Geneva, the chief canton of entrance from France, asked the Federal Council for relief from this burden. The Council suggested that Geneva try suit for reimbursement against the canton of citizenship. Geneva followed this advice, and the Tribunal gave the redress asked, *Geneva v. Bern* (1924), saying that if these persons

had arrived from another canton in such condition that they could not travel farther, Geneva certainly would not have had to carry the costs of their medical care and burial and, if it did incur them, would be able to recover, not from their home canton, to be sure, but from the canton in whose territory [they were when] the illness became severe. The fact that they came not from another canton but from France, is no sufficient reason for putting the burden on Geneva.

When a person falls ill abroad and the foran state, rightly or wrongly, fails to provide necessary medical aid, it is, as a general principle, the duty of his home state to help him; and in the case of a Swiss citizen this means his home canton. Geneva . . . in caring for them . . . is acting in lieu . . . of their home canton. . . . Hence a legal relation . . . is established like that of "gestion d'affaires" (justified performance of another's business) in civil law, the rules of which apply by analogy.

So the Tribunal allowed the recovery on this basis of unjust enrichment despite a federal statute which expressly said that it was every canton's duty to take care of any indigent confederal (temporarily) unable to travel and despite the general rule that allows suit for reimbursement only if the canton of citizenship has been notified that its cantonal is in *permanent* need and has refused to receive him back or remit the costs of his care.

The United States Supreme Court has never been asked to

grant poor relief reimbursement between states; tho such claims between towns or counties within many states are handled by courts. Why this system does not exist between state and state I find unexplainable. The absence of inter-state (federal common) law respecting public assistance leaves a gap. This gap has, in the last thirty years, been partly, but not completely, filled by *federal* "categorical aids," that is, programs providing cash and other benefits to all who suffer certain of the more frequent causes of destitution—old age, total disability, death of wage-earner, blindness, etc. But gaps remain that leave migrants and casuals to the irregular mercy of private charity; gaps which now and then have tragic consequences.

This difference between the countries in dealing with this interstate problem seems to have no connection with the variances in substantive law—that Swiss poor relief falls to the canton (or commune) of citizenship, American to the state (or town) of settlement; that Swiss law affords the specific alternative of compulsory return home of indigents in permanent need and American law pretty clearly forbids this as a deprivation of personal liberty; that a canton into which an indigent is unlawfully expelled by another can recover against the expelling canton, and no such rule has yet been recognized in the United States. Tho controversies as to which state is liable for caring for a particular person or family in distress indeed often occur, I have found no example of their settlement by judicial decision, either in the Supreme Court in suits between states or in any other court between political units of different states. Would not such a process be convenient? Perhaps, despite absence of constitutional or statutory provisions for settlement of interstate liability for public assistance, it is time for a daring state to try such a suit. For, tho it is true that a pervasive absence of a common law duty of states to support those in need and of the corresponding right of all people within the state to be saved from starvation and cared for in illness, which is the foundation of the Swiss law of cantonal reimbursement for such expenditures for confederals, is characteristic of American law; yet, even if in American law succor is owed only to residents gaining settlement, if it is provided by another state to such persons, as may often occur in the case of migrant workers or transient vacationers, the state of settlement could properly be required to reimburse the state that provides it; and the Court should, it seems, entertain such suits against the state of settlement by any other state supplying it; as, on the other side of the ocean, the Tribunal has widened by interpretation the narrow provisions of the Constitution and statutes relating to assistance to indigents.

The Tribunal also has had to define the boundaries of poor relief. Take the case of *Vaud v. St. Gallen* (1950), concerning liability for care of an indigent citizen of Vaud who, while in St. Gallen, was found to be an habitual drunkard and was committed to a St. Gallen reformatory. Here the question brought to Lausanne for judgment was not whether the relief needed was for a permanent disability, but whether support of a person so committed was a form of poor relief or of punishment (the cost of which may not be exacted from the canton of citizenship). St. Gallen might have tested the matter by suing Vaud when Vaud refused to reimburse St. Gallen for his support. Instead, St. Gallen by administrative order prepared to send him back to Vaud, as the Swiss law permits in the case of indigents if the home canton refuses to supply support. So Vaud went to the Federal Tribunal to quash the deportation order and vindicate Vaud's refusal to pay. The Tribunal said the outcome depended on whether this administrative internment was analogous to hospitalization or to imprisonment. Deciding that it was "a measure of social care" and not a punishment, the court held that the cost of it was an expense for which the home canton (Vaud) must pay or else accept the patient's repatriation.

On the other hand a duty of reimbursement, characteristic of the law of poor relief, may be carried by contract into other areas. Cantons have thus undertaken to pay for the keep of their indigent citizens convicted of crime in another canton. (For the keep of the nonindigent prisoner, he himself has to pay.) So it was between Zurich and St. Gallen when, in 1943, they litigated concerning liability for Vogel imprisoned in Zurich. But there was a complicating factor: Vogel, while under sentence, renounced his St. Gallic citizenship. The Tribunal, without deciding whether the relation between Vogel and St. Gallen was effectively ended by Vogel's unilateral act, was persuaded by Zurich to hold that the paticular agreement between the cantons lasted for the duration of the sentence which had been imposed before his change of citizenship. Nor did it say whether, if, after finishing his prison term, he was indigent, St. Gallen would still have an obligation of support.

6 NONTERRITORIAL
LITIGATION
OF THE LAST CENTURY
IN THE UNITED STATES

INTERCANTONAL cases often involve what the Restatement of Foreign Relations Law of the American Law Institute calls the state's "capacity to enforce" the law relating to a particular person, thing, or transaction. The Swiss law is inclined to single out one canton as having such capacity while the American law often recognizes several states as having a connection with the person, thing, or transaction sufficient to justify enforcement—judicial or administrative application of this law—by any one of them.

Statutes of certain types are applied only by the courts or executive agencies of the state that enacts the statute. Thus in punishment of crime the state that has capacity to prescribe what is criminal is usually the only one with capacity to enforce this law. (But in twentieth-century Helvetia the prosecution of offenders against federal penal law is left largely to *cantonal* prosecutors and *cantonal* courts.) Internationally, and likewise between members of the American federation, usually a state enforces only its own criminal law. By extradition the accused person who is elsewhere is brought back for the process of enforcement to the state whose prescription he broke. We have seen that a similar device—compulsory return—may be used by a canton responsible for economic assistance to its indigent citizen living in another canton.

Again as to taxation, capacity to enact and capacity to

collect are customarily tied together. State A enforces only what state A has enacted and uses only the administrative and judicial agencies of state A to do so. (But there is now a start of enforcement thru courts of one state of tax liability imposed by the law of another.) Expropriation is another matter handled ordinarily only by the executive and judicial agencies of the state authorizing it. Another is escheat (taking by the state of ownerless property). Workmen's accident compensation in the United States follows this pattern; and so does divorce—the administrative or judicial machinery of each state is geared to give effect only to the law of that state.

In many matters, however, the courts of a state apply the law prescribed by other states where deemed appropriate. Which other state in any particular case? The question of "choice of law" or "conflict of laws" is different from the question of "capacity to enforce," "choice of administration," or "conflict of competences." It is in these conflicts of competences between cantons that the Swiss Federal Tribunal has far more active traffic in interstate cases than the Supreme Court.

Indeed one might have said until recently that no case—with the doubtful exception of *Texas v. Florida* (1939)—avowedly between states, that turns on an issue of conflict of competences other than conflict as to geographic boundaries, has elicited a Supreme Court opinion. But there is no doubt that *Texas v. New Jersey* (1965) was a case of this sort—a conflict between several states, each claiming power to escheat the same property, to take to itself specific intangible wealth of which the owner could not be found.

Of course issues of choice of law and issues of choice of administration, both, are constantly litigated in the United States, and lower court decisions on these issues are constantly reviewed by the Supreme Court. The absence or rarity of state-against-state cases is no token of harmony between the states on such issues. They may, for example, be settled by suits in which the plaintiff is a private person and the defendant a state officer or agency trying to exercise a control which, the plaintiff asserts, may not be exercised by that state.

With the foregoing caution that an examination of cases
before the Supreme Court between states does not provide a
full spectrum of competence issues which, substantially, are
litigated between states, let us turn to the interstate cases of
the last century that involve issues other than those of territorial and quasiterritorial rights covered in Chapter 4.

Before there were any such cases between states Pennsylvania's objection to obstruction of interstate navigation outside the boundaries of the complaining state had been upheld
in a suit which it brought against a private person
[*Pennsylvania v. Wheeling Bridge Co.* (1851)]. With the
exception of *Kentucky v. Dennison* (1861), analyzed in earlier chapters, it was not till 1876 that the Supreme Court
decided a case between *states* that was other than a boundary
controversy. In that year South Carolina failed in a suit
against Georgia for violating a compact between them by
which Georgia promised freedom of navigation of the Savan-
nah River. After the compact was negotiated, the United
States had erected a dam in Georgia which diverted the water
in that river in the interest of interstate and international
commerce. The Court of course held that the federal power
was paramount, compact or no compact, and Georgia was not
liable for this interference with freedom of navigation. A
federal statute likewise ultimately defeated Pennsylvania in
the *Wheeling Bridge* case (1856).

A quarter century later the plaintiff state was no more
successful when Louisiana sued Texas (1900) to annul a
Texas prohibition of the import of goods into Texas from
New Orleans, Louisiana, to prevent spread of yellow fever.
Referring to the *Wheeling Bridge* case to distinguish it as
"one to protect property . . . of Pennsylvania" (tho the plaintiffs in both suits mainly complained of obstruction of private
commerce), the Court denied Louisiana standing to sue,
deeming individuals the only persons whose rights were possibly infringed. For this and other reasons, to me even less
persuasive, the complaint was dismissed.

Contract rights (payment of defendant state's bonds) were
the subject of suit in *New Hampshire v. Louisiana* and *New
York v. Lousiana,* decided together in 1883—the only other

nonboundary cases between states decided in the nineteenth century—and also in *South Dakota v. North Carolina* (1904). The nub of the controversy was the Eleventh Amendment. The Court held that it protected a state from being sued on a bond sold to and owned by a private person, even tho he had authorized his state to collect for him, but did not prevent suit on a bond of which the plaintiff state is beneficial owner, even tho its ownership had been acquired from a private owner of the bond. This result of course applies the principle that states, except for their immunity from suit, are liable on their promises made by contract as well as by compact, a principle which no judge questioned. The contention was over the reach of the immunity from suit established by the Eleventh Amendment. The defendant accordingly prevailed in the earlier cases, but South Dakota won a 5 to 4 decision in 1904, the first instance in which a state succeeded in a claim for money against another, or indeed any claim other than for territory.

A much larger contract or compact claim was involved in *Virginia v. West Virginia,* a case started in 1906 and not finally disposed of until 1918, in which Virginia demanded that West Virginia pay a fair share of the public debt of the Commonwealth of Virginia that existed at the time of West Virginia's separation from the Commonwealth early in the Civil War. The obligation was recognized in the new state's constitution as well as in the resolution of the legislature of the "Restored State of Virginia" or "Restored Government of the Commonwealth" (representing the part of the Commonwealth within Union military lines, most of which became West Virginia) consenting to the separation. In a series of nine decisions (1907–1918) the Court sustained its jurisdiction, dealt with the merits of the claim, determined its amount, and finally considered how payment of the judgment, which it had pronounced and which the West Virginia legislature had refused to pay, should be exacted, a problem which was dissipated in 1918 by West Virginia's acceptance of the obligation.

Suits over diversion and pollution of waters (including marginal ocean), have been reviewed in an earlier chapter.

But it should be added that *North Dakota v. Minnesota* (1923) recognized that a state may obtain preventive redress against another state for diversion of water into a boundary lake alleged to have caused damaging floods in the plaintiff's territory and loss to it as a landowner; but the Court refused redress because it found no causal action by Minnesota; and it rejected also the claim for damages for losses suffered by other landowners in North Dakota both for this reason and also because, as in *New Hampshire v. Louisiana*, this was deemed a private claim, from which the Eleventh Amendment immunized the defendant state. Since this claim was the principal ground of suit, the Court allowed Minnesota costs against North Dakota (1924). In boundary cases, the Court said, costs were ordinarily divided between the states, but this rule "does not apply to cases in which the parties have a litigious interest." Somewhat similarly recovery of costs from a canton is restricted to cases in which its pecuniary liability is in issue [Swiss Judicature Act, Art. 156].

A similar distinction between rights of states and rights of individuals, at least to a money judgment, was made by the Swiss Federal Tribunal, when, in Ticino's suit against Graubünden (1923), tho it prohibited the defendant's taxing of plaintiff's citizens in Graubünden because they were only sojourners there, it refused to allow Ticino to recover taxes they had already paid, because that claim was a "private law" right of reimbursement of the taxpayers, not a right of the plaintiff canton.

Another essentially interstate case relating to a compact of states bordering the Ohio River for the preservation of its cleanliness came to the Court by the appellate route, *West Virginia v. Sims* (1951). Justice Frankfurter in writing the Court's opinion pointed out that here the states had wisely chosen to negotiate a compact, a way of settling "regional controversies" that is preferable to "contentious litigation before this Court." Tho this suit concerning "the meaning and validity of compacts" reached the Court by another route than "by way of an original action brought by a state," the same rules of law applied, the justice said. Reserving the question whether an explicit state constitutional prohibition of delegating legislative power to an interstate agency (which had been done by this compact) would be honored above a compact (with which reservation some of the justices did not agree), he found no difficulty in reconciling a *general* implication in the West Virginia constitution of nondelegability of legislative power with the *specific* terms of the compact, and accordingly enforced these terms. Some years earlier (1914) the Swiss Tribunal had before it a case in which it upheld a statute of Bern as more potent than a compact between Bern and Neuchâtel that had never received Bernese legislative approval and therefore was, by the law of Bern, unconstitutional. (It was Neuchâtel that sought and obtained this judgment that the compact was by Bernese law invalid.)

Not referred to in surveying American boundary cases, was a case concerning the effect of political control on title to underwater land, which needs mention. Massachusetts asserted title but not jurisdiction against the State of New York and the City of Rochester in an area formerly under Lake Ontario but now become shoreland. The Supreme Court, construing the Treaty of Hartford of 1786 between the two states, concluded (1926) that the title to certain riparian land which New York thereby recognized to be in Massachusetts did not extend to land under water at that time and that the title to such land was, almost necessarily, attached to the imperium over the lake area which by the treaty Massachusetts recognized to be in New York.

Alabama in 1934 was denied leave to sue to stop Arizona and other states from prohibiting sale in the respective states of goods made by prisoners of Alabama. The Court stated many objections, none convincing to me—that a single suit complaining of statutes, however similar, of several states, was multifarious (an improper joinder of a variety of complaints), was trivial, and was brought by a plaintiff without standing to complain because it had suffered, and was likely to suffer, no direct harm. (All Alabama's prison industry was operated by a contractor, who then sold the product.) The opinion, citing *Louisiana v. Texas* (1900), went so far as to say that the Court would not exert its jurisdiction in inter-state controversies "in the absence of extreme necessity."

A controversy concerning rights under a compact between New Jersey and Pennsylvania for the construction of a boundary river bridge was fought out in two cases in 1940, one brought by Pennsylvania against New Jersey in the Supreme Court, and the other, appealed from the New Jersey courts, brought by a landowner near the bridge against the Bridge Commission appointed by the two states. A bit of the Supreme Court's opinion in the appellate case has been quoted in Chapter 3, and that opinion served also to dispose of the case between the states.

In *Arkansas v. Texas* (1953) the University of Arkansas was recognized as an arm of the state with standing to sue another state. It had made a contract with a Texas corporation and brought suit to prevent Texas from interfering with the corporation's performance of the contract, which Texas by Texas litigation was trying to prevent as ultra vires—beyond the legal powers—of the corporation under Texas law. At the first stage—on motion for leave to file the suit—a majority of the Court deferred action to await the outcome of the Texas litigation. Four judges wanted to be done with the case at once. All apparently agreed that if the contract was held ultra vires by the Texas court, Arkansas' case would fail. The case proceeded no further, being settled, and Arkansas was let withdraw (1956) her motion for leave.

Alabama was denied leave to file a suit against Texas (1954) to prevent the operation of a statute of Congress vesting or revesting in the seaboard states rights in the area sometimes called "tidelands," but improperly, for it was land under the marginal sea between low-tide line and the outer limits of the maritime belt of territorial waters. These rights had been held to belong to the United States in a series of decisions referred to at the end of Chapter 4, which Congress had overruled. In denying leave, the Court expounded the substantive law upholding the validity of the statute, and said nothing about Alabama's standing as a plaintiff, tho it seems doubtful.

In 1958 when California sought to sue Washington to prevent taxation of California wines more heavily than Washington wines, the Court expounded the substantive constitutional law (Twenty-first Amendment) that permits such discrimination and denied leave to file.

Interstate litigation broke into a new area in 1965—that of escheat.

Escheat in England was the taking by the Crown of lands without an owner. This practice has in the United States been extended by statute to all property of a person who dies without disposing of it by will and without kin empowered by statute to inherit it. And by recent statutes states have been thus expropriating other unclaimed property. New Jersey applied escheat to dividends owing to undiscoverable shareholders of New Jersey corporations. That state, in its own court, sued such a corporation, the Standard Oil Company, and obtained judgment requiring payment to the state of such dividends. The company carried the case to the Supreme Court, which in 1951, by a 5 to 4 vote, affirmed the recovery. The dissenters thought the potential claims of other states were not disposed of in a suit in which they were not parties; thus the defendant might have to pay again. But the majority, finding no pretension by any other state, held that New Jersey had a better right than the Standard Oil Company to this windfall, and was not deterred by the possibility that some other state might have a stronger claim than New Jersey. The minority's anxiety spread during the next ten years as many states enacted escheat statutes. So in *Western Union Telegraph Co. v. Pennsylvania* (1961) (also an appellate case) the Court ordered the dismissal of Pennsylvania's suit to escheat undeliverable credits created by senders (of money telegrams) within and without the state for transmittal to addresses in Pennsylvania, saying that the absence of New York, the corporation's state of birth, and other possible claimant states, made any decision improper. The escheatable intangible thus became a bone of contention between several states that had some connection with the debtor or the creditor, under escheat statutes which embrace unclaimed deposits in banks within the enacting state, un-

claimed inheritances from estates of decedents adminis-
tered in the enacting state's courts, and other apparently
ownerless property.

What link of such intangibles with a state was crucial for
the state to claim them by statutory escheat?

In a third case, *Texas v. New Jersey and other states*
(1965), the Court (with Justice Black writing) decided the
issue, for that case at least, in favor of the state of the
creditor—that is, the state of his last address shown on the
books of the debtor. The Court recognized that it was laying
down a new rule. How sweeping a rule it is, is yet to be
determined. Here small claims (dividends, etc.), owed by the
Sun Oil Company, were the subject of escheat. New Jersey
was the state of incorporation; but the Court (over a dissent
by Justice Stewart) rejected New Jersey's claim based on this
link. It also rejected the demand of the state within which
the debtor created the claim or that within which the creditor
created the claim, in favor of that of the state of the creditor's
last known address (as shown in the records of the debtor, to
avoid difficulty of proof). This disposed of most of the
claims, but not all; New Jersey, the state of incorporation,
was awarded claims of creditors of undiscoverable address
and of creditors whose address is a state that does not provide for "escheat or custodial care" of such unclaimed credits.
Whatever the best solution of this conflict of competences
may be, and however much or little the solution found in
Texas v. New Jersey may supersede the rules for escheat of
decedents' estates, of bank accounts, and of other claims, for
which a different rule of attribution has become settled without interstate controversy, it is at least clear that this type of
controversy is suitable for legal determination in suits between competing states. Tho without an exact Swiss counterpart, it is a controversy of a type within the Swiss tradition of
settlement of competence conflicts by adjudication between
cantons.

Such is the variety of the interstate litigation in the United
States during the last hundred years. It is noteworthy how
rarely the plaintiff has won the battle.

7 SWISS CASES NOT RELATED TO TERRITORY OR PUBLIC ASSISTANCE

I N the Swiss Federal Tribunal the record of success for the plaintiff is more normal than in the United States Supreme Court, and cases are more numerous and more varied.

We have about one-tenth of the Tribunal's decisions available in print, as nine-tenths are never published. The annual index of all cases disposed of indicates that not over 10 percent of cases between cantons are thus made available to the public. From year to year, the number of decisions and of reported decisions varies; and changes in statistics don't always reflect true changes. Thus, there was a marked increase (to 27) in the number of completed cases between cantons listed in the 1963 index. (None of the 27 was reported, however.) Nearly all involved "double taxation," it appears, in which an individual assessed by two or more cantons on the same property asked for a determination of which canton was entitled to tax him. Cases of this type have become frequent in recent years, but they had not till 1963 been indexed as cases between cantons. Their true character is now acknowledged by the additional listing of them as such. But 1963 in fact showed no notable increase of these cases or of all cases between one canton and another.

When the Swiss Tribunal started actively to settle disputes between cantons in 1875, the brevity of its institutional history, compared with that of the Supreme Court, which was already eighty-five years old, was compensated by a long and strong tradition among the cantons of peaceful settlement of political disputes, a more consistent practice of conciliation and arbitration of such issues than in any other part of the world. This characteristic background of the modern judicial handling of intercantonal disputes has been described by William Bross Lloyd, Jr., in his booklet *Waging Peace, the Swiss Experience* (1958), and I have briefly referred to it, in its relation to adjudication, in *Law among States in Federacy* (1959), at pages 301–310.

The practice persists in current litigation; for the Tribunal normally attempts to mediate when it sees hope of thus avoiding adjudication. So in the contest over the custody of an illegitimate child, *Obwalden v. Zurich* (1949), the Tribunal, as its opinion states, had unsuccessfully "tried in Luzern to bring a settlement about by conferring with representatives of the executive councils and wardship authorities of the parties and in the presence of the guardian, the foster parents and the mother of the child." No doubt such efforts, often made by lower courts in both countries and sometimes by referees appointed by the Supreme Court in interstate cases, tho they deprive us of the delineation of much fascinating law, save the litigants time and money. Yet there may be a difference of opinion whether the same persons who will have to adjudicate if their mediation fails should have these rather different responsibilities.

The Federal Tribunal in response to cantonal demand often assures cooperation between cantons in the administration of justice, by declaring and defining duties of cantonal officers, usually executive officers, in this area of "judicial assistance."

In the enforcement of criminal law, the Swiss practice is more effective than what has been developed from the language of the United States Constitution. *Kentucky v. Dennison* (1861) blighted a growth that should have been favored by the Supreme Court. In *Solothurn v. Uri* (1910) the Tribunal said that, whatever the obligation between international states because of lack of confidence of one state in the administration of law elsewhere, "within a federal state there should be no room for such lack of confidence, not even if the material and formal criminal law of the individual members does not always agree in content, as in the case of Switzerland."

Since then, criminal substantive and procedural law has been almost completely federalized; but judicial assistance is still needed because the law's administration is very largely by cantonal prosecutors and cantonal courts.

The tendency to nationalize the criminal law in the United States is marked both by proliferating federal offenses, tho not of course to the Swiss degree, and by providing some opportunity for defendants to remove state prosecutions for state offenses to United States courts for trial [*Tennessee v. Davis* (1879)]. A big enlargement of this opportunity was denied, however, by the Supreme Court's interpretation of civil right statutes in *Greenwood v. Peacock* (1966).

Tho the duty to extradite an accused between cantons and to give other forms of judicial assistance is now set by federal statute and nourished by judicial decision, litigation still is frequent because of disagreement as to which cantons should handle particular cases, now no longer a question of common law but one of interpretation of a federal statute. The Code of Penal Procedure empowers the federal Department of Justice and Police to make this decision, but the Code does not make its decision always final. The Federal Tribunal has the last say. In *Ticino v. Zurich* (1956), the Ticino prosecutor objected successfully to the Department's assignment of a certain case to it. In some instances, of course, a canton may seek to try a particular case.

Such controversies involve conflict of competences rather than judicial assistance—a negative conflict in the *Ticino* case, as in many public assistance cases, for each canton disclaims the burden.

Among the many cases concerning enforcement of the penal law, one of the most peculiar was that brought by Luzern against Nidwalden (1927) when Nidwalden refused to make an investigation requested by Luzern to assist in prosecuting a person for fishing without a Luzern license in an area of the Lake of the Four Forest Cantons that was in dispute between the plaintiff and the defendant. One might have expected that this controversy would require the Tribunal to decide where the boundary was, but, since neither canton requested this, the issue did not arise, the court said. The controversy was disposed of by a holding that so long as the boundary remained in dispute and so long as there was no sufficient practice to establish de facto sovranty in Luzern, there was no violation of law in Nidwalden's refusal. The Tribunal added: "This decision does not mark any absence of law regarding fishing. Luzern was and is always free to bring the boundary controversy before the Federal Tribunal and at the same time to ask for the application of proper protective [interim] measures." Today fishing rights in the area are still in negotiation, but the boundary in other respects has been set by a compromise accepted by the two cantons (1962–1963).

We have glanced at the administration of the criminal law. Cooperation between cantons in applying civil law also is mandatory, for the principle of intercantonal judicial assistance pervades all Swiss law; and issues concerning cooperation or conflict over certain phases of it—administration of estates of decedents and incompetents, for example—often are settled by litigation between appropriate organs of cantons.

An example of a civil law conflict is supplied by a controversy between the Orphans' Office of Krummenau, a town of St. Gallen, and that of Wädenswil, a town of Zurich (1945)—*St. Gallen v. Zurich*, for short—over the custody of a feeble-minded German domiciled in Switzerland. The only issue was the interpretation of a federal statute regarding change of domicil of incompetents. In this type of case between towns of different cantons, as in litigation between the cantons themselves (that is, their executive councils), the Federal Tribunal is a court of first instance. Discord over such power to administer, it has said, even when it relates to private law matters, "wears the dress of public law" [*Zurich v. Geneva* (1925)]. It is a matter of cooperation with and deference to the canton that has the right or the duty to act. In *Zurich v. Geneva*, Geneva was willing to leave a prostitute at large whom Zurich had declared incompetent and had committed to an institution, from which she had escaped. As a domiciliary of the plaintiff—tho a citizen of Aargau—she was subject to its control, and, tho no extradition statute applied, Geneva was required to send her back to Zurich. A sort of fugitive slave law? No; but an expression of the idea that just as woman's place is in the home (for, except in a few cantons, Swiss women are still voteless), so an incompetent's is within his own domicil. Compare the ruling of *Schaffhausen v. Thurgau* (1940) that, when a widow marries and the family needs public assistance, the children of the first marriage, if of another cantonal allegiance than that of their stepfather, are subject to separation from their mother and her present husband and repatriation. In 1928 the Rural Basel Execution and Bankruptcy Authority sued successfully to compel a court of Bern to enforce a fine lawfully imposed on a Bernese lawyer by the Authority. Not a suit between cantons of the usual type, it did not originate in the Federal Tribunal. But the decision is a good example of giving effect to the duty of intercantonal cooperation, ancillary to bankruptcy, a civil proceeding.

The intercantonal tax cases all concern not cooperation but conflict among cantons. Their number is legion, for the Tribunal is vigilant in the application of a provision of the Constitution which, tho calling for legislation which has never been enacted, has as full effect as have several clauses of the Fourteenth Amendment and other prohibitions of the United States Constitution not supported by statutes. The Swiss Constitution, Article 46, says that the legislature *shall* provide for the prevention of double taxation; the American, that it *may* provide for the carrying out of the requirements imposed on states by the Fourteenth and other amendments. But in both countries, without legislation the courts enforce these constitutional standards by denying effect to cantonal (state) statutes that transgress them.

Such provisions (especially in international treaties),

whether negative or positive, are often called self-executing—or more properly self-legislating. In a sense they are the opposite of "political questions." Here the courts apply the constitutional (or treaty) rule without executive or legislative mediation tho the matter might be thought one that needs first such political action; in contrast, the political question is one which the courts will not touch, because they deem it to need legislative or executive definition before any issue can exist that is proper for judicial settlement.

The Swiss court is often moved to such action by a canton which disputes the right of another canton to tax a person with respect to specific property or a specific transaction or event that the plaintiff claims to be within its own taxing realm and therefore, by the rule against multiple taxation, outside the taxing realm of the defendant or any other canton. For example, Luzern sued Aargau (1921) to determine which could tax a truck that was used in both cantons; Zurich sued Luzern (1930) to determine which was entitled to administer (and tax) the estate of a woman whose domicil at death was disputed; Thurgau sued St. Gallen (1954) and got the court (after it had asked the opinion of all cantons) to overrule earlier cases and hold that a minor who is employed and lives in another canton than his parents' home has a tax domicil where he lives, tho his civil domicil remains with his parents. Rural Basel sued Urban Basel (1937) to determine whether the latter could collect a tax to finance unemployment compensation from employers in the city canton on wages paid for work done there by employees who lived outside it.

While in the United States the prohibition of multiple taxation of *tangible* property and, to some extent, of transactions and events that have contact with more than one state is, so far as it reaches, held to rest on several constitutional provisions, including due process of law, no enforcement of it by suit between states has yet occurred. Nor could there be enforcement by another type of suit, mentioned earlier in this chapter, which is frequent in Helvetia—suit brought by a taxpayer against two or more cantons to determine which is entitled to tax him, such as *Straub v. St. Gallen and Thurgau* (1951) concerning an estate tax, the issue being the domicil of the decedent.

In the United States there is the difficulty that mere man may not sue his majesty the state; and a further difficulty that whom-do-I-owe litigation (interpleader) is generally allowed only where the plaintiff acknowledges that he owes a specific amount, and the dispute is only as to who is his creditor, while in a tax conflict, one state's claim may be very different in amount from the other's because of their various tax laws.

Indeed even if one of the cantons levies no tax, in which case conflict between them is in a sense absent, there may still be conflict concerning jurisdiction to tax, which is sufficient in Swiss law. Such a contest is described as one over "fiscal sovranty" [*Egger v. Bern and Graubünden* (1959) (fully reported in the *Journal des Tribunaux*, but not in the official reports)]. Whether this sovranty is presently exercised is irrelevant. Thus the Tribunal said in *Odermatt v. St. Gallen Catholic Tax Authority* (1943) that there is a violation of the prohibition of "double taxation" in Article 46 of the Constitution, "Whenever one canton by laying a tax intrudes into the tax jurisdiction reserved to another even if the latter makes no use of it." And it was argued in *Ticino v. Graubünden* (1923) and apparently agreed by the Tribunal that an excessive charge to a confederal (for a license to sojourn in a canton) would be prohibited because its excess would make it "really and properly a tax in violation of Article 46 instead of a temporary residence fee not repugnant to it."

The Tribunal recognizes that the rule must not be extremely extended [*Messner v. Zurich* (1952)]; but it is firmly established and repeatedly applied to many sorts of taxes. Speaking of a tax on gain from sale of land, situated in a canton where the owner was not domiciled, the Tribunal said in *F. v. Zurich and other cantons* (1957): "Federal rules concerning conflicts apply not only against actual but also against potential double taxation; they forbid intrusion into the tax sovranty of another canton." And this view was taken concerning a corporation tax in *X. v. Ticino* (1960).

Tho *actual* conflict is not required in taxation cases, the Tribunal has ruled the other way in conflicts of penal sovranty involving crimes "prosecuted only upon charge," that is, minor crimes. Thus in *Ticino v. Zurich* (1947) the Tribunal said: "there cannot be any conflict of competence between cantons as long as the cantonal authorities alleged to have jurisdiction [to prosecute] have not been invoked," as those of Zurich had not, tho they had been apprised of the facts.

This sample of Swiss tax cases has few American analogs. Indeed only one case, involving the estate of the son of the renowned Hetty Green, is much like the countless Swiss cases—*Texas v. Florida and other states* (1939), where assets were insufficient to satisfy the estate tax claims of the several claimant states. The Supreme Court here granted redress. But, speaking by Chief Justice Hughes, it soon denied it in another tax case, *Massachusetts v. Missouri* (1939), because "Missouri is not injuring Massachusetts . . . and recovery by either [of its tax] does not impair the exercise of any right the other may have."

Texas' suit, the earlier by a few months, is carefully distinguished. Of the later case the Chief Justice said: "It is not shown that the tax claims of the two states are mutually exclusive. On the contrary the validity of each claim is wholly independent of that of the other. . . . The question is thus different from that presented in *Texas v. Florida,* where the controlling consideration was that by the law of the several States concerned only a single tax could be laid by a single State, that of domicile."

The ground of the almost contemporaneous *Texas-Florida* decision, as here explained, is not conflict of competences in the Swiss sense, for the law involved is described not as federal law, but as "the law of the several States." More important, the relief was not posited on the conflict of these laws alone, but, as the Chief Justice saw it, on the fact that

"It also appeared that there was danger that through success-ful prosecution of the claims of the several States in inde-pendent suits enough of the estate would be absorbed to deprive some State of its lawful tax." That is, more than the whole estate might be found by the several states to be due as taxes from the estate of a decedent whom each state found to be its resident. This potential loss of tax revenue in *Texas v. Florida* was the focus of the opinion of the Court by Justice (later Chief Justice) Stone, who said that "the risk that decedent's estate might constitutionally be subjected to con-flicting assessments in excess of its total value and that the right of complainant or some other State might be defeated" was what led the Court to examine and declare in what state he was domiciled at death. This the Court decided to be Massachusetts.

But Massachusetts, the laureate in *Texas v. Florida,* failed in her suit against Missouri, already pending, to persuade the Court to act, tho the two states had similar reciprocal statutes (but there was no compact between them) concerning prop-erty taxed in another state. For, said Chief Justice Hughes, "the enactment of so-called reciprocal legislation cannot be regarded as conferring on Massachusetts any contractual right [or as creating] an obligation which either State is entitled to enforce against the other in a court of justice."

Settlement of a conflict of tax competences in *Texas v. Florida* has had no tax litigation successor; but the escheat cases discussed in the preceding chapter are at least collat-eral heirs.

Not all Swiss tax cases between cantons involve a conflict of tax competences. If the Confederation levies a tax and distributes it to the cantons according to some formula, dis-pute may arise between them as to the meaning or applica-tion of the federal statute—a conflict of claims but hardly of competences. A controversy about such a tax on corporations was adjudicated in 1919 between Nidwalden and Luzern. Another such case settled in 1949 a controversy concerning the military-service-exemption tax paid by Dr. Descoeudres, an unmarried physician of Neuchâtel cantonality, a medical missionary in Asia, who returned to his parents' home in Geneva from time to time. The federal statute provided that the money go to the canton of the taxpayer's domicil, or, if he have no Swiss domicil, to the canton of his citizenship. The issue here, as also in many competence conflict cases, was, where was his domicil; and the Tribunal found that since Descoeudres had not stayed at any place abroad to the extent of making it his home, "the center of his life," the plaintiff Neuchâtel was not entitled to the tax money, for Geneva was his domicil.

The exercise of federal legislative power often makes inter-cantonal jurisdictional controversies take the shape of controversies over the construction of a federal statute. But they remain controversies settlement of which may be effectuated by litigation among cantons. Indeed now most suits between cantons or between the Confederation and cantons involve construction of specific language of the Constitution or the federal statutes or intercantonal compacts.

THE TALE'S END

LOOKING over the nearly one hundred years of reported public law adjudication between Swiss cantons, we see that the major concern of these suits has shifted: from boundaries and judicial cooperation, to water use control and jurisdiction over incompetents and responsibility for public assistance to the poor, and from those subjects to competence to tax and to prosecute. In the United States during the same period the tide of cases concerning boundary disputes waxed and ebbed, amplified by some concerning water use. But otherwise the types of cases of Swiss concern have had few American counterparts; and vice versa.

In both countries boundary controversies are diminishing, probably because few boundaries remain vague; so are water use cases, because to a large extent control has been turned over by national legislation to national executive agencies. The number of poor-relief cases between Swiss cantons is decreasing because, by compact between most cantons, settlement of those that involve permanent indigence has been transferred from the Tribunal to the federal Department of Justice and Police without recourse to courts. The almost complete nationalization of the Swiss penal law has lessened the rank, and probably the rancor, of conflicts over competence to prosecute. But over competence to tax, where no federal statute operates, the cantons continue to wage courtly battle.

A miscellany of cases on other topics in both countries lightly sprinkles the reports; in the United States they have rarely yielded profit to the plaintiff party. But no reason is obvious for the slight use in the United States of the interstate suit as a means of settling affirmative conflicts over competence to apply laws relating to certain types of state taxation and negative conflicts over competence to carry out state laws relating to public assistance. The Swiss amplitude of the legal duty of judicial assistance between cantons is being developed in the United States by the general adoption of various "uniform laws"—if new distrust or dislike does not arise from strong differences between states concerning methods of dealing with wrongdoers, especially the use of the death penalty.

The Supreme Court has, I think, used excessive caution in its handling of cases between states. The "leave to file" a suit marks interstate litigation as "made to order" for each suitor. But suits in the court like suits in the clothing shop should be on the rack, ready to wear for the state that needs one—as they are in Helvetia.

The Supreme Court concerns itself too much with protecting the defendant state from possible harassment by litigation, perhaps overlooking that in the exercise of its original jurisdiction states are more often plaintiffs than defendants, and that by rejecting their suits in limine it diminishes the political stature of states who knock at its august portal. A generous recognition of their parental standing as suitors would be not only prestigious but also practically beneficial, in my opinion.

Admittedly much interstate litigation is a transitional device between the international law conception of the state as protector and champion of all its people and the modern way of letting every man be his own protagonist in litigation even against states. Yet international states and constituent states of a federacy are and should never cease to be plaintiffs—or defendants—with regard to their own property, and their own conduct as legal persons who make contracts and perform duties and have rights.

The ending of the defendant state's suit-immunity should reduce the plaintiff state, as protector or champion, to the modest role of a city or of a labor union or other voluntary group, which, at least in the United States, is recognized to be at times a fit champion of its citizens or its members, as, for instances, the Supreme Court of Wisconsin held in *Associated Hospital Service v. Milwaukee* (1961), and the Supreme Court of the United States in *National Motor Freight Traffic Association v. United States* (1963). But so long as, in the United States, the doctrine of state immunity from private suit retains some vigor, the Supreme Court could well be more friendly to complaints by one state against another, not only to heighten the standing of the plaintiff but also to prevent the defendant from escaping from liability for failing to do its proper share in building a mature relationship of federation and domestic peace thru law.

The Supreme Court's present reluctance to give redress, which Professor Bickel has dubbed a passive virtue, takes many forms between states—some of which we have only glanced at: (1) that the plaintiff state lacks standing or is not the "real party in interest" and so is incompetent to obtain redress; (2) that the issue is political or legislative rather than legal, a hurdle which the Court boldly lept in *Rhode Island v. Massachusetts* (1838) for territorial disputes, but by which it was as notably daunted in *Kentucky v. Dennison* (1861); (3) that the dispute is not "ripe" for judicial consideration; (4) that the wrong is not of "serious magnitude"; (5) that the evidence for the state seeking relief is not more than preponderant.

These obstacles the Swiss Federal Tribunal has not erected, at least not so explicitly. Instead it has seen in intercantonal litigation an effective and everyday tool for preventing gaps and overlaps between the constituent states in exercising their limited sovranty. If a country wishes to live under a rule of law without such centralization and standardization as damps the moral and cultural individuality of the states, judicial control of the boundaries of competence of the states appears to be no less important than judicial delimitation of geographic boundaries between them. *Texas v. New Jersey* (1965) perhaps shows that such an idea can flower in the New World too. It is an area where the suit of state-against-state may well become a normal mode of settlement.

From this survey of cases adjudicated by the highest courts of two federal states, may we not conclude at least that settlement by law by such organs is a good way to proceed? For this system has proved to be a significant factor in the maintenance of peace thru law both among the erstwhile pugnacious Germanic communities of the central highlands of Europe and among the component states of the most industrially and militarily exuberant country of the modern world, a country roughly comprising all the land, between Canada and Mexico, that surfaces the quarter of this Earth east of the international date line.

That federations can live successfully without such a practice, however, is proved even from the evidence we have examined—from the fact that, except for territorial boundary and water-flow cases, there is little coincidence in the two federacies of the areas in each in which interstate litigation is a usual course for solving problems between member states.

The due judicial *process* that is so highly desirable where so powerful suitors as states meet in controversy, may be practiced by nonjudicial bodies. And however suitable for use in the decision of such conflicts are legal *standards*, they too may be loyally, tho a little crudely, applied by nonjudicial bodies. Moreover, as everyone agrees, some disputes between intrafederational states should be settled by politics rather than by law, these political settlements often taking legal form in federal statutes, interstate compacts, or constitutional amendments. Yet all in all, it seems to me, Switzers and Americans together may fitly boast that not only modern federalism but also the method of settlement of disputes between component units of federacies by a standing court administering law, has been born in the United States in the New World, and in Helvetia in the Old World, and that, with the somewhat different personalities of their highest courts, these two systems have prospered, each in its own habitat.

An essential virtue of courts is their collegiality. For collegiality is the right matrix both for creating or prescribing law in general terms and for applying or enforcing law in specific situations (at least where the controversy is between major antagonists). Indeed Switzerland presses preference for group action in government so far as to have its executive authority also collegial.

The word "court" itself manifests this essence. Derived from the Latin *cohors*, it means a group. The royal court has always meant the *group* around the king; the Great and General Court (of Massachusetts) is the legislature; and the English Courts of King's Bench and of Common Pleas were groups of men learned in the common law. I think as good a case can be made for the primarily collegial meaning of the words *Gericht* and *Tribunal*.

Today in the United States we hear both court and cohort perverted to refer to a single person. "Comrade" has apparently been so smirched with the connotation of communism, and "collaborator" with that of nazism that now, instead of comrades or collaborators, an individual companion in some enterprise is often dubbed a cohort! Likewise a single judge calls himself and is called a court. (One would like to read the term as a courteous inclusion with the judge of the jury, or perhaps the bailiff and the clerk; but one cannot, for the word court has now become a sort of editorial or royal "we," consisting of one black-robed figure.) Yet I maintain that a true court, no less than a cohort, is many-manned and that this (recognized in the almost universal provision for appeal to a bench of several judges) is its greatest virtue as an ultimate decider between great contenders. This virtue is of course assured in the handling of interstate disputes; for them the high court, composed of many judges, is at once the initial and the ultimate trier. Perhaps a high court whose standards are not purely legal—whatever that elusive term may mean—composed of members whose training and experience are not tightly legal, might be as satisfactory for the maintenance of peace and order and justice between states bound in federacy. The job might be done by the national legislature, as to some extent it still is in Switzerland, or—the national legislature having a great load to carry without this—by a board of arbitrators, standing or ad hoc, not composed exclusively of lawyers and not professing to apply law alone. But an essential of the success of any organ of settlement certainly is plurality of membership.

There is no reason, however, to remake or replace the excellent organs of settlement that the Swiss and the American federal republics have. In the Swiss Tribunal, intercantonal litigation is normal legal business of one legal person in controversy with another. To treat it otherwise in the United States by a highly individualized procedure and by hurdles hindering plaintiff states may not be the best way of affording adjustment with other states of a federacy that will give all these states the LEX, IUSTITIA, PAX, proclaimed on the entablature of the Palais du Tribunal fédéral in Lausanne, or the EQUAL JUSTICE UNDER LAW, similarly displayed in Washington. Characterized by these means and goals, adjudication is honored by both countries as tending to assure a happy and stable relationship among their member states no less than among all other persons within their boundaries; and the experience of each for a century or more is an impressive record of continuing realization of the hopes with which provisions for settlement of interstate controverses by litigation in the highest court were built into their respective constitutions.

APPENDIX 1 EXCERPTS FROM THE CONSTITUTION OF THE UNITED STATES

ARTICLE 1, SECTION 10:

No State shall enter into any Treaty, Alliance or Confederation, . . .

No State shall, without the Consent of Congress . . . enter into any Agreement or Compact with another State, or with a foreign Power, . . .

ARTICLE 3, SECTION 2:

The judicial Power shall extend . . . to all Cases affecting Ambassadors, . . . to Controversies to which the United States shall be a Party;—to Controversies between two or more States;—between a State and Citizens of another State; . . .

In all Cases affecting Ambassadors, other public Ministers and Consuls, and those in which a State shall be a Party, the Supreme Court shall have original Jurisdiction. In all other Cases . . . appellate Jurisdiction . . . with such Exceptions and under such Regulations as the Congress shall make.

ARTICLE 4, SECTION 1:

Full Faith and Credit shall be given in each State to the public Acts, Records and Judicial Proceedings of every other State. . . .

ARTICLE 4, SECTION 2:

A Person charged in any State with . . . Crime, who shall flee from Justice, and be found in another State, shall on demand of the executive Authority of the State from which he fled, be delivered up to be removed to the State having Jurisdiction of the Crime.

AMENDMENT 11:

The Judicial power of the United States shall not be construed to extend to any suit . . . prosecuted against one of the United

117

States by Citizens of another State or by Citizens or Subjects of any Foreign State.

AMENDMENT 14, SECTION 1:

All persons born or naturalized in the United States and subject to the jurisdiction thereof, are citizens of the United States and of the State wherein they reside. No State shall make or enforce any law which shall abridge the privileges and immunities of citizens of the United States; nor shall any State deprive any person of life, liberty or property, without due process of law; nor deny to any person within its jurisdiction the equal protection of the laws.

AMENDMENT 14, SECTION 5:

The Congress shall have power to enforce, by appropriate legislation, the provisions of this article.

AMENDMENT 21, SECTION 2:

The transportation or importation into any State, Territory, or possession of the United States for delivery or use therein of intoxicating liquors, in violation of the laws thereof, is hereby prohibited.

APPENDIX 2   EXCERPTS FROM THE CONSTITUTIONS AND STATUTES OF SWITZERLAND

THE CONSTITUTION OF 1848*

ARTICLE 40. Execution of final judgments in civil cases rendered in any canton may be levied thruout Switzerland.

[Art. 61 of the present Constitution is the same.]

ARTICLE 55. Federal legislation shall provide for extradition of accused persons from one canton to another; but it may not be made obligatory for political offenses or those of the press.

[Art. 67 of the present Constitution is substantially the same.]

ARTICLE 74. Within the authority of the two councils [i.e., the two houses of parliament] are:

.   .   .   .

16. Controversies between cantons relating to public law.

[Art. 83 of the present Constitution corresponds with this article but omits this heading.]

ARTICLE 101. As a court of civil law, the Federal Tribunal adjudicates:

1. Provided they do not relate to public law, controversies:
   a) between cantons
   b) between the Confederation and a canton.

.   .   .   .

In cases under heading 1 . . . the matter is brought to the Tribunal by action of the Federal Council. If the Council decides that it is not within the Tribunal's competence, the controversy is decided by the Federal Assembly [i.e., the two houses of parliament.]

[Art. 110 of the present Constitution omits the second paragraph and restates the part quoted from the first paragraph without substantial change.]

* Trans. William G. Rice.

119

THE CONSTITUTION OF 1874*

ARTICLE 7. All separate alliances and all treaties of a political character between Cantons are forbidden.

On the other hand, Cantons have the right to conclude conventions among themselves upon matters of legislation, administration, and justice. In all such cases they are to bring the conventions to the cognizance of the Federal authorities, who shall prevent their being executed if they contain anything repugnant to the Confederation or to the rights of other Cantons. If there is no repugnancy, the Cantons are entitled to claim from the Federal authorities co-operation in the execution of such conventions.

ARTICLE 9. In special cases, the Cantons retain the right of concluding treaties with foreign Powers upon the subjects of public economic regulation, cross-frontier intercourse, and police relations; but such treaties shall contain nothing repugnant to the Confederation, or to the rights of other Cantons.

ARTICLE 10. Official relationships between a Canton and a foreign Government or its representatives take place through the intermediacy of the Federal Council.

Nevertheless, upon the subjects mentioned in Article 9, the Cantons may correspond directly with the interior authorities and the officials of a foreign State.

ARTICLE 16. In cases of internal disturbance, or if danger is threatened from another Canton, the government of the Canton threatened shall give immediate notice to the Federal Council, so that the latter may, within the limits of its competences (Article 102, ss. 3, 10, 11), take the necessary measures or summon the Federal Assembly. In urgent cases the [cantonal] government in question is authorized to seek the help of other Cantons, which are bound to afford it. The Federal Council must be at once informed. . . .

ARTICLE 43. Every citizen of a Canton is a Swiss citizen. . . .

ARTICLE 45. Every Swiss citizen has the right to obtain settlement in any part of Swiss territory provided he is in possession of a Certificate of Origin or similar document.

In exceptional cases settlement may be refused, or may be withdrawn from, those who as a consequence of a criminal sentence are not in enjoyment of civil rights.

Furthermore, settlement may be withdrawn from those who have been repeatedly sentenced by the Courts for serious criminal offences, as well as from those who are a permanent charge on

---

* As now in force; trans. Christopher Hughes, *The Federal Constitution of Switzerland* (1954). Since neither Hughes nor A. J. Peaslee, *Constitutions of Nations* (1950), is consistent in his translations—e.g., the German *Niederlassung* or French *établissement* is sometimes "settlement," sometimes "residence," sometimes "domicil"—I have used my own translation in discussing these articles in the text.

public charity and to whom the commune or Canton of origin, as the case may be, refuses adequate support after having been officially requested to afford it. . . .

ARTICLE 46. In matters of civil law persons settled in Switzerland are as a general rule subject to the jurisdiction and to the legislation of the place where they reside.

Federal legislation shall lay down the provisions necessary in order to give effect to this principle, and to prevent Double Taxation.

ARTICLE 61. Final judgments in civil cases pronounced in one Canton can be executed anywhere on Swiss territory.

ARTICLE 67. Federal legislation shall make the necessary provision for extradition of accused persons from one Canton to another; nevertheless extradition may not be made compulsory for political or press offences.

ARTICLE 102. The principal powers and obligations of the Federal Council, within the limits of the present Constitution, are as follows:

1. It conducts the affairs of the Confederation, in accordance with Federal Laws and *arrêtés*.
2. It sees to the observance of the Constitution and the Laws and *arrêtés* of the Confederation and the provisions of Federal concordats: it takes the necessary action to see that they are obeyed, either acting on its own initiative or in response to an appeal against a grievance, unless the appeal is of the type which should go before the Federal Tribunal under Article 113. . . .

ARTICLE 110. The Federal Tribunal decides civil law disputes:

1. between the Confederation and a Canton;
2. between the Confederation on the one side and corporations or private persons on the other, provided that the latter are the plaintiffs and the amount in dispute is of the value which Federal law stipulates;
3. between Cantons;
4. between a Canton on the one side and corporations or private persons on the other, at the instance of one or other of the parties and when the amount in dispute is of the value which Federal law stipulates.

The Federal Tribunal further decides cases concerning *Heimatlosat* and disputes upon 'citizenship' between communes of different Cantons.

ARTICLE 113. The Federal Tribunal takes cognizance also of:

1. conflicts of competence between Federal authorities on one side and Cantonal authorities on the other side.
2. disputes in public law between Cantons.
3. appeals against violation of constitutional rights of citizens, and appeals of private persons against violation of concordats or international treaties.

Administrative disputes as determined by Federal legislation are excepted.

In all the above cases the Federal Tribunal shall apply the Laws and the universally binding *arrêtés* passed by the Federal Assembly, and the treaties which it has ratified.

ARTICLE 114 *bis*. The Federal Administrative Court takes cognizance of those classes of Federal administrative conflict which Federal legislation shall transfer to it.

The Administrative Court also has jurisdiction in those disciplinary cases which Federal legislation refers to it, unless they are referred to a special tribunal instead. . . .

THE JUDICATURE ACT*

ARTICLE 22.1. Judges, substitute judges, representatives of the ministry [i.e., attorneys general], magistrates, scribes, and jurors must not serve

a) In a case which directly concerns themselves [or near relatives].

b) In a case in which they have participated previously [in specified capacities].

c) In a case in which their home canton or town is a party or may be indirectly liable.

ARTICLE 41. The Federal Tribunal has original jurisdiction

a) Of civil law controversies between the Confederation and a canton or between cantons.

ARTICLE 83. The Federal Tribunal has jurisdiction

a) Of conflicts of competence between federal authorities on the one hand and cantonal authorities on the other.

b) Of public law controversies between cantons when a cantonal government invokes it and the matter is not one within the competence of the Federal Council because of special provisions of federal legislation.

c) [Of controversies about citizenship]

d) [Of controversies between authorities of different cantons over application of the federal statute concerning residence by confederals]

e) [Of like controversies about wardship]

ARTICLE 156.1. In general [in public and civil law cases] court costs are borne by the losing party.

2. Ordinarily court costs may not be imposed on the Confederation, the cantons, or the towns when, unless a money recovery is involved, they are in court in performance of their official functions or in support of their official actions.

* *Loi fédérale d'Organisation judiciaire.* Trans. William G. Rice.

Case	Cases Adjudged in the Supreme Court	Supreme Court Reporter	U.S. Reports Lawyers' Edition	Page references in this book
Alabama v. Arizona (1934)	291 U.S. 286	54 S. Ct. 399	78 L. Ed. 798	57, 96
Alabama v. Georgia (1860)	64 U.S. (23 How.) 505	. . . .	16 L. Ed. 556	71, 72
Alabama v. Texas (1954)	347 U.S. 272	74 S. Ct. 481	98 L. Ed. 689	81, 97
Alabama v. United States (1963)	371 U.S. 37	83 S. Ct. 145	9 L. Ed. 2d 112	8
Arizona v. California (1931)	283 U.S. 423	51 S. Ct. 522	75 L. Ed. 1154	76, 78
Arkansas v. Tennessee (Mar. 1918)	246 U.S. 158	38 S. Ct. 301	62 L. Ed. 638	73
—— (June 1918)	247 U.S. 461	38 S. Ct. 557	62 L. Ed. 1213	"
—— (1925)	269 U.S. 152	46 S. Ct. 31	70 L. Ed. 206	"
—— (1926)	271 U.S. 629	46 S. Ct. 634	70 L. Ed. 1122	"
Arkansas v. Tennessee (1940)	310 U.S. 563	60 S. Ct. 1026	84 L. Ed. 1362	22, 26, 49, 59, 97
Arkansas v. Texas (1953)	346 U.S. 368	74 S. Ct. 109	98 L. Ed. 80	97
—— (1956)	351 U.S. 977	76 S. Ct. 1042	100 L. Ed. 1493	97
Baker v. Carr (1962)	369 U.S. 186	82 S. Ct. 691	7 L. Ed. 663	28, 39, 40
Banco Nacional v. Sabbatino (1964)	376 U.S. 398	84 S. Ct. 923	11 L. Ed. 2d 804	42
California v. Washington (1958)	358 U.S. 64	79 S. Ct. 116	3 L. Ed. 2d 106	98
Cherokee Nation v. Georgia (1831)	30 U.S. (5 Pet.) 1	. . . .	8 L. Ed. 25	56, 67, 68
Chisholm v. Georgia (1792)	2 U.S. (2 Dall.) 419	. . . .	1 L. Ed. 440	18, 19
Clark v. Barnard (1883)	108 U.S. 436	2 S. Ct. 878	27 L. Ed. 780	19
Colorado v. Kansas (1943)	320 U.S. 383	64 S. Ct. 176	88 L. Ed. 116	59, 77, 78
—— (1944)	322 U.S. 708	64 S. Ct. 1043	88 L. Ed. 1552	58
Colson v. Lewis (1817)	15 U.S. (2 Wheat.) 377	. . . .	4 L. Ed. 266	58
Connecticut v. Massachusetts (1931)	282 U.S. 660	51 S. Ct. 286	75 L. Ed. 602	57, 59, 76, 78
Craig v. Missouri (1830)	29 U.S. (4 Pet.) 410	. . . .	7 L. Ed. 903	66

Case	Cases Adjudged in the Supreme Court	Supreme Court Reporter	U.S. Reports Lawyers' Edition	Page references in this book
Delaware River Joint Toll Bridge Comm. v. Colburn (1940)	310 U.S. 419	60 S. Ct. 1039	84 L. Ed. 1287	48, 58, 97
Florida v. Georgia (1855)	58 U.S. (17 How.) 478	. . . .	15 L. Ed. 181	39, 71
Georgia v. Penn. R.R. (1945)	324 U.S. 439	65 S. Ct. 716	89 L. Ed. 1051	12, 26
Georgia v. Tennessee Copper Co. (1907)	206 U.S. 230	27 S. Ct. 618	51 L. Ed. 1038	12, 54, 80
Georgia R.R. & Banking Co. v. Redwine (1952)	342 U.S. 299	72 S. Ct. 321	96 L. Ed. 335	19
Governor of Georgia v. Madrazo (1828)	26 U.S. (1 Pet.) 110	. . . .	7 L. Ed. 73	38
Greenwood v. Peacock (1966)	384 U.S. 808	86 S. Ct. 1800	16 L. Ed. 2d 944	102
Hinderlider v. LaPlata Ditch Co. (1938)	304 U.S. 92	58 S. Ct. 803	82 L. Ed. 1202	31, 58, 59, 77
Hopkins Loan Association v. Cleary (1935)	296 U.S. 315	56 S. Ct. 235	80 L. Ed. 251	12
Iowa v. Illinois (1893)	147 U.S. 1	13 S. Ct. 239	37 L. Ed. 55	73
Kansas v. Colorado (1902)	185 U.S. 125	22 S. Ct. 552	46 L. Ed. 838	12, 39, 51, 76, 77, 78
—— (1907)	206 U.S. 46	27 S. Ct. 655	51 L. Ed. 956	51, 58, 76, 77, 78
Kansas v. Missouri (1944)	322 U.S. 213	64 S. Ct. 975	88 L. Ed. 1234	74
Kansas v. United States (1907)	204 U.S. 331	27 S. Ct. 388	51 L. Ed. 510	50
Kentucky v. Dennison (1861)	65 U.S. (24 How.) 66	. . . .	16 L. Ed. 717	37, 39, 40, 43, 71, 93, 101, 112
Kentucky v. Indiana (1930)	281 U.S. 163	50 S. Ct. 275	74 L. Ed. 784	49

Case	Cases Adjudged in the Supreme Court	Supreme Court Reporter	U.S. Reports Lawyers' Edition	Page references in this book
Lake Level Case. *See* Wisconsin v. Illinois				
Louisiana v. Mississippi (1906)	202 U.S. 1	26 S. Ct. 408	50 L. Ed. 913	75
Louisiana v. Mississippi (1966)	384 U.S. 8	86 S. Ct. 1250	16 L. Ed. 2d 330	71, 72, 75
Louisiana v. Texas (1900)	176 U.S. 1	20 S. Ct. 251	44 L. Ed. 347	41, 57, 93, 96
Louisiana v. United States (1965)	380 U.S. 145	85 S. Ct. 817	13 L. Ed. 2d 709	8
Marbury v. Madison (1803)	5 U.S. (1 Cranch) 137	. . . .	2 L. Ed. 60	18
Maryland Committee for Fair Representation v. Tawes (1964)	377 U.S. 656	84 S. Ct. 1442	12 L. Ed. 2d 595	29
Massachusetts v. Mellon (1923)	262 U.S. 447	43 S. Ct. 597	67 L. Ed. 1078	26
Massachusetts v. Missouri (1939)	308 U.S. 1	60 S. Ct. 39	84 L. Ed. 3	33, 107
Massachusetts v. New York (1926)	271 U.S. 65	46 S. Ct. 357	70 L. Ed. 838	96
Minnesota v. United States (1939)	305 U.S. 382	59 S. Ct. 292	83 L. Ed. 235	28
Minnesota v. Wisconsin (1920)	252 U.S. 273	40 S. Ct. 313	64 L. Ed. 558	73
Missouri v. Illinois (1901)	180 U.S. 208	21 S. Ct. 331	45 L. Ed. 497	12, 79
—— (1906)	200 U.S. 496	26 S. Ct. 268	50 L. Ed. 572	59, 79
Missouri v. Iowa (1849)	48 U.S. (7 How.) 660	. . . .	12 L. Ed. 861	71, 75
Missouri v. Kentucky (1871)	78 U.S. (11 Wall.) 395	. . . .	20 L. Ed. 116	71
Monaco v. Mississippi (1934)	292 U.S. 313	54 S. Ct. 745	78 L. Ed. 1282	19, 67
National Motor Freight Traffic Assoc. v. United States (1963)	372 U.S. 246	83 S. Ct. 688	9 L. Ed. 2d 709	112
Nebraska v. Wyoming (Apr. 1935)	295 U.S. 40	55 S. Ct. 568	79 L. Ed. 1289	76
—— (Dec. 1935)	296 U.S. 553	56 S. Ct. 369	80 L. Ed. 390	77

APPENDIX 3 TABLE OF CASES ADJUDGED IN THE UNITED STATES SUPREME COURT
(Continued)

Case	Cases Adjudged in the Supreme Court	Supreme Court Reporter	U.S. Reports Lawyers' Edition	Page references in this book
Nebraska v. Wyoming (1938)	304 U.S. 545	58 S. Ct. 1035	82 L. Ed. 1519	77
—— (1945)	325 U.S. 589	65 S. Ct. 1332	89 L. Ed. 1815	59, 76, 77, 78
New Hampshire v. Louisiana (1883)	108 U.S. 76	2 S. Ct. 176	27 L. Ed. 656	50, 56, 93, 95
New Jersey v. Delaware (1934)	291 U.S. 361	54 S. Ct. 407	78 L. Ed. 847	72, 73
New Jersey v. New York (1831)	30 U.S. (5 Pet.) 284	. . . .	8 L. Ed. 127	64
New Jersey v. New York (1931)	283 U.S. 336	51 S. Ct. 478	75 L. Ed. 1104	59, 78
New Jersey v. New York City (1931)	283 U.S. 473	51 S. Ct. 519	75 L. Ed. 1176	12, 54, 80
New Jersey v. Sargent (1926)	269 U.S. 328	46 S. Ct. 122	70 L. Ed. 289	56
New York v. Connecticut (1799)	4 U.S. (4 Dall.) 1	. . . .	1 L. Ed. 715	63
New York v. Louisiana. See New Hampshire v. Louisiana				
New York v. New Jersey (1921)	256 U.S. 296	41 S. Ct. 492	65 L. Ed. 937	80
New York v. O'Neill (1959)	359 U.S. 1	79 S. Ct. 564	3 L. Ed. 2d 585	42
Nielson v. Oregon (1909)	212 U.S. 315	29 S. Ct. 383	53 L. Ed. 528	35
North Dakota v. Minnesota (1923)	263 U.S. 365	44 S. Ct. 138	68 L. Ed. 342	55, 57, 59, 95
—— (1924)	263 U.S. 583	44 S. Ct. 208	68 L. Ed. 461	95
Ohio v. West Virginia. See Pennsylvania v. West Virginia				
Oklahoma v. Atchison Ry. (1911)	220 U.S. 277	31 S. Ct. 434	55 L. Ed. 465	12
Oklahoma v. Texas (1921)	256 U.S. 70	41 S. Ct. 420	65 L. Ed. 831	72, 73, 75
Pawlet v. Clark (1815)	13 U.S. (9 Cranch) 292	. . . .	3 L. Ed. 735	58
Pennsylvania v. New Jersey (1940)	310 U.S. 612	60 S. Ct. 1084	84 L. Ed. 1389	48, 58, 97
Pennsylvania v. West Virginia (1923)	262 U.S. 553	43 S. Ct. 658	67 L. Ed. 1117	8, 12, 54, 80

Case	Cases Adjudged in the Supreme Court	Supreme Court Reporter	U.S. Reports Lawyers' Edition	Page references in this book
Pennsylvania v. Wheeling Bridge Co. (1851)	54 U.S. (13 How.) 518	. . . .	14 L. Ed. 249	93
—— (1856)	59 U.S. (18 How.) 421	. . . .	15 L. Ed. 435	93
Rhode Island v. Massachusetts (1838)	37 U.S. (12 Pet.) 657	. . . .	9 L. Ed. 1233	37, 38, 64, 68, 69, 70, 74, 112
—— (1846)	45 U.S. (4 How.) 591	. . . .	11 L. Ed. 1116	38, 68
South Carolina v. Georgia (1876)	93 U.S. 4	. . . .	23 L. Ed. 782	75, 93
South Carolina v. Katzenbach (1966)	383 U.S. 301	86 S. Ct. 803	15 L. Ed. 769	8, 29
South Dakota v. North Carolina (1904)	192 U.S. 286	24 S. Ct. 269	48 L. Ed. 448	50, 94
Standard Oil Co. v. New Jersey (1951)	341 U.S. 428	71 S. Ct. 822	95 L. Ed. 1078	98
Tennessee v. Davis (1879)	100 U.S. 257	. . . .	25 L. Ed. 648	102
Texas v. Florida (1939)	306 U.S. 398	59 S. Ct. 563	83 L. Ed. 817	33, 92, 107
Texas v. New Jersey (1965)	379 U.S. 674	85 S. Ct. 626	13 L. Ed. 2d 596	36, 92, 99, 113
Texas v. New Mexico (1939)	308 U.S. 510	60 S. Ct. 118	84 L. Ed. 435	59
United States v. Alabama (1960)	362 U.S. 602	80 S. Ct. 924	4 L. Ed. 2d 982	8
United States v. California (1947)	332 U.S. 19	67 S. Ct. 1658	91 L. Ed. 1889	35, 81
United States v. Louisiana (1950)	339 U.S. 699	70 S. Ct. 914	94 L. Ed. 1216	81
United States v. Mississippi (1965)	380 U.S. 128	85 S. Ct. 808	13 L. Ed. 2d 717	8
United States v. Oregon (1935)	295 U.S. 1	55 S. Ct. 610	79 L. Ed. 1267	81
United States v. Texas (1892)	143 U.S. 621	12 S. Ct. 488	36 L. Ed. 285	31

Case	Cases Adjudged in the Supreme Court	Supreme Court Reporter	U.S. Reports Lawyers' Edition	Page references in this book
United States v. Texas (1896)	162 U.S. 1	16 S. Ct. 725	40 L. Ed. 867	31, 75, 81
United States v. Texas (1950)	339 U.S. 707	70 S. Ct. 918	94 L. Ed. 1221	81
United States v. Utah (1931)	283 U.S. 64	51 S. Ct. 438	75 L. Ed. 844	31, 57, 81
United States v. West Virginia (1935)	295 U.S. 463	55 S. Ct. 789	79 L. Ed. 1546	56
Vermont v. New Hampshire (1933)	289 U.S. 593	53 S. Ct. 708	77 L. Ed. 1392	72
Virginia v. Tennessee (1893)	148 U.S. 503	13 S. Ct. 728	37 L. Ed. 537	50
Virginia v. West Virginia (1870)	78 U.S. (11 Wall.) 35	....	20 L. Ed. 67	39, 71
Virginia v. West Virginia (1907)	206 U.S. 290	27 S. Ct. 732	51 L. Ed. 1068	48, 53, 66, 94
—— (1908)	209 U.S. 514	28 S. Ct. 614	52 L. Ed. 914	", ", ", "
—— (Mar. 1911)	220 U.S. 1	31 S. Ct. 330	55 L. Ed. 353	", ", ", "
—— (Oct. 1911)	222 U.S. 17	32 S. Ct. 4	56 L. Ed. 71	", ", ", "
—— (1913)	231 U.S. 89	34 S. Ct. 29	58 L. Ed. 135	", ", ", "
—— (1914)	234 U.S. 117	34 S. Ct. 889	58 L. Ed. 1243	", ", ", "
—— (1915)	238 U.S. 202	35 S. Ct. 795	59 L. Ed. 1272	", ", ", "
—— (1916)	241 U.S. 531	36 S. Ct. 719	60 L. Ed. 1147	", ", ", "
—— (1918)	246 U.S. 565	38 S. Ct. 400	62 L. Ed. 883	", ", ", "
Tassel v. Georgia (1831?)	....	....	....	64
Washington v. Oregon (1936)	297 U.S. 517	56 S. Ct. 540	80 L. Ed. 837	59, 77
Wesberry v. Sanders (1964)	376 U.S. 1	84 S. Ct. 526	11 L. Ed. 2d 481	29
Western Union Tel. Co. v. Pennsylvania (1961)	368 U.S. 71	82 S. Ct. 199	7 L. Ed. 2d 139	98
West Virginia ex rel. Dyer v. Sims (1951)	341 U.S. 27	71 S. Ct. 557	95 L. Ed. 713	80, 95

APPENDIX 3 TABLE OF CASES ADJUDGED IN THE UNITED STATES SUPREME COURT
(Concluded)

Case	Cases Adjudged in the Supreme Court	Supreme Court Reporter	U.S. Reports Lawyers' Edition	Page references in this book
Wisconsin v. Illinois (Lake Level Case) (1929)	278 U.S. 367	49 S. Ct. 163	73 L. Ed. 426	53, 79
—— (1930)	281 U.S. 179	50 S. Ct. 266	74 L. Ed. 799	" "
—— (1933)	289 U.S. 395	53 S. Ct. 671	77 L. Ed. 1283	" "
—— (1940)	311 U.S. 107	61 S. Ct. 154	85 L. Ed. 73	" "
Wisconsin v. Michigan (1935)	295 U.S. 455	55 S. Ct. 786	79 L. Ed. 1541	73
Worcester v. Georgia (1832)	31 U.S. (6 Pet.) 515	. . . .	8 L. Ed. 483	65
Wyoming v. Colorado (1922)	259 U.S. 419	42 S. Ct. 552	66 L. Ed. 999	78
Wyoming v. Colorado (1932)	286 U.S. 494	52 S. Ct. 621	76 L. Ed. 1245	" "
—— (1936)	298 U.S. 573	56 S. Ct. 912	80 L. Ed. 1339	
Wyoming v. Colorado (1940)	309 U.S. 572	60 S. Ct. 765	84 L. Ed. 954	65

APPENDIX 4 TABLE OF CASES ADJUDGED IN THE SWISS FEDERAL TRIBUNAL

Case	Arrêts du Tribunal fédéral vol.	part	page	Journal des Tribunaux vol.	part	page	Page references in this book
Aargau v. Solothurn (1892)	18		689				78
Aargau v. Solothurn (1915)	41	I	126				80
Aargau v. Thurgau, Appenzell (1950)	76	IV	265	1951 JdT	IV	42	33
Aargau v. Zurich (1878)	4		34				75, 78
Confederation v. Urban Basel (1939)	65	I	106	1939 JdT	I	493	8, 42
Confederation v. Zurich (1965)							34
Egger v. Bern, Graubünden (1959)	85	I	7	1960 JdT	I	54	106
F. v. Zurich, other cantons (1957)	83	I	329				106
Fribourg v. Federal Council (1952)	78	I	14				24, 51, 76
Geneva v. Bern (1924)	50	I	125				25, 87
Geneva v. Confederation (1955)	81	I	35	1956 JdT	I	572	31
Geneva v. Urban Basel (1927)	53	I	309	1928 JdT	I	230	86
Graubünden v. Ticino (1892)	18	I	673				36
Gut v. Luzern, Nidwalden (1955)	81	I	264	1956 JdT	I	90	33
Juzi v. Bern, Schaffhausen (1948)	74	I	273				9, 10, 33
Luzern v. Aargau (1882)	8		43				35
Luzern v. Aargau (1921)	47	I	509	1922 JdT	I	501	105
Luzern v. Neuchâtel (1947)	73	I	230	1948 JdT	I	47	26, 85
Luzern v. Nidwalden (1927)	53	I	300	1928 JdT	I	118	35, 37, 44, 102
Luzern v. Zug, Geneva (1945)	71	I	89	1945 JdT	I	454	33
Luzern Probate Authority v. Vaud (1928)	54	I	119				45, 54
Messner v. Zurich (1952)	78	I	417	1953 JdT	I	108	106
Neuchâtel v. Bern (1914)	40	I	550				96
Neuchâtel v. Confederation (1879)	5		520				42
Neuchâtel v. Geneva (1949)	75	I	200	1950 JdT	I	220	106
Nidwalden v. Luzern (1919)	45	I	37	1919 JdT	I	311	108
Obwalden v. Zurich (1949)	75	I	139	1950 JdT	I	78	45, 55, 101

APPENDIX 4 TABLE OF CASES ADJUDGED IN THE SWISS FEDERAL TRIBUNAL
(Continued)

Case	Arrêts du Tribunal fédéral			Journal des Tribunaux			Page references in this book
	vol.	part	page	vol.	part	page	
Odermatt v. St. Gallen (1943)	69	I	225	1944 JdT	I	152	35, 106
Outer Appenzell v. St. Gallen (1895)	21	I	957				36
Rural Basel v. Urban Basel (1937)	63	I	147	1938 JdT	I	499	31, 105
Rural Basel Execution & Bankruptcy Authority v. Bern (Court of Neuveville) (1928)	54	I	106	1929 JdT	II	165	45, 104
Sagitta Co. v. Solothurn (1958)	84	I	150	1959 JdT	I	220	80
Schaffhausen v. Thurgau (1940)	66	I	165	1940 JdT	I	563	104
Schaffhausen v. Zurich (1897)	23	I	1405				36, 72, 74
Schwyz v. Uri (1908)	34	I	274				35
Schwyz v. Uri (1951)							35
Schwyz v. Zurich (1926)	52	I	170				76, 77
Solothurn v. Aargau (1900)	26	I	444				9, 12, 54, 55, 80, 81
Solothurn v. Uri (1910)	36	I	49				101
St. Gallen v. Thurgau (1913)	39	I	56				84
St. Gallen v. Zurich (1945)	71	I	158	1945 JdT	I	374	103
Straub v. St. Gallen, Thurgau (1951)	77	I	22	1952 JdT	–	154	106
Thurgau v. St. Gallen (1928)	54	I	188				35
Thurgau v. St. Gallen (1954)	80	I	184	1954 JdT	I	600	105
Ticino v. Graubünden (1923)	49	I	131	1923 JdT	I	474	9, 10, 95, 106
Ticino v. Zurich (1947)	73	IV	205	1948 JdT	IV	28	107
Ticino v. Zurich (1956)	82	IV	121	1956 JdT	IV	153	102
Urban Basel v. Fribourg (1951)				1952 JdT	I	372	26, 86
Urban Basel v. Solothurn (1882)	8	I	436				25, 83
Urban Basel v. Solothurn, Rural Basel (1952)	78	I	346	1933 JdT	I	600	33
Uri v. Schwyz (1915)	41	I	511				35

APPENDIX 4   TABLE OF CASES ADJUDGED IN THE SWISS FEDERAL TRIBUNAL
(Concluded)

Case	Arrêts du Tribunal fédéral			Journal des Tribunaux			Page references in this book
	vol.	part	page	vol.	part	page	
Valais v. Zurich (1945)	71	I	233	1945 JdT	I	578	45
Vaud v. St. Gallen (1950)	76	I	104	1951 JdT	I	120	89
X. v. Ticino (1960)	86	I	209	1961 JdT	I	111	107
Zug v. Schwyz (1901)	....		....	....			36
Zurich v. Geneva (1925)	51	I	309	....			48, 84, 103
Zurich v. Glarus (1928)	54	I	328	1929 JdT	I	489	49, 74
Zurich v. Luzern (1930)	56	I	450	1931 JdT	I	541	105
Zurich v. St. Gallen (1943)	69	I	243	1944 JdT	I	330	89
Zurich v. St. Gallen (1955)	81	I	143	....			9, 10
Zurich v. Schaffhausen (1907)	33	I	537	....			35, 72, 74
Zurich v. Schaffhausen (1917)	43	I	303	....			36, 86
Zurich v. Thurgau (1914)	40	I	409	....			84

APPENDIX 5 TABLE OF OTHER CASES

Associated Hospital Service v. Milwaukee (1961) 13 Wis. 2d 447 (p. 469) 109 NW2d 271 (p. 281); referred to in this book on p. 112.

In re Cooper (1960) 53 Cal. 2d 772, 349 P2d 956; referred to in this book on p. 42.

Gulley v. Apple (1948) 213 Ark. 350, 210 SW2d 514; referred to in this book on p. 42.

Pennsylvania v. Connecticut (1782) (no opinion); referred to in this book on p. 63.

Schroeder v. Freeland (1951) 188 F2d 517; referred to in this book on p. 68.

South West Africa Cases (1966), I.C.J. Reports 1966, p. 6; referred to in this book on pp. 40, 56.

Trail Smelter Case (U.S. v. Canada) (1938 and 1941) *American Journal of International Law,* Vol. 33, p. 182, and Vol. 35, p. 684; referred to in this book on pp. 55, 79.

Victoria v. Commonwealth of Australia (1957) 99 C.L.R. 575; referred to in this book on p. 8.

Württemburg, Prussia v. Baden (1927) *Entscheidungen des Reichsgerichts in Zivilsachen,* Vol. 116, App. p. 18; referred to in this book on p. 78.